Wm. G. Justice

DMin, DPhil, DLitt

Damned
If We Are Not
Forgiven

Understanding Guilt
and People Who Are
Their Own Worst Enemies

GlobalEdAdvancePress
37321-7635 USA

Damned If We Are Not Forgiven
Understanding Guilt and People Who Are Their Own Worst Enemies

Library of Congress Control Number: 2008927836

   Justice, William G., 1930–
      Damned If We Are Not Forgiven
      ISBN 978-0-9796018-9-6
      Subject Codes and Description: 1: REL012070 Religion:
      Christian Life - Personal Growth 2: REL019000 - Religion:
      Counseling 3: REL075000 0- Religion: Psychology of
      Religion

Printed in the United States of America

Published by
GlobalEdAdvancePress
37321-7635 USA

Dedicated

To the memory of
Ann
My wife

and
Mary and Gross Justice
My parents

and
To my Lord

All of whom have taught me
About guilt and the
Grace of forgiveness

Other Books by Author

Don't Sit on the Bed
(A Handbook for Visiting the Sick)

Guilt and Forgiveness
(How God Can Help You Feel Good About Yourself)

Guilt, the Source and the Solution
(Defense Systems to Avoid Feeling Guilty)

When Death Comes
(A Handbook for Pastors and Laypersons
Who Minister to the Bereaved)

When Your Patient Dies
(A Handbook for Physicians and Nurses
Who Minister to Families at the Time
of a Patient's Death)

Jesus' Silent Years:
Exploring Facts the Gospels Do Not Tell Us

God in the Hands of Angry Sinners

Jesus the Maverick King

The Nature of God as Revealed in Jesus

Training Guide for Visiting the Sick

When God Seems Silent

Contents

PREFACE

You have experienced feelings of guilt. People all around you have experienced them. (The few people who have not experienced feelings of guilt are in prison or probably are headed there.) Feelings of guilt are painful and you don't want to live with it. You want release.

I had been a professional hospital chaplain, professional counselor, and marriage and family therapist for roughly twenty years when I wrote my first book on guilt: Guilt and Forgiveness. Soon afterward, I wrote a second book on the subject, Guilt: the Source and the Solution (see Bibliography). That was roughly twenty-seven years ago. Having served as a professional hospital chaplain and as a licensed professional counselor, over a period of forty-five years, I listened to approximately 300,000 persons at the hospital bedside and behind the closed doors of the counseling office. Guilt is often unrecognized, even by professional therapists. Yet, it continues to extract a price from physical, mental, and spiritual health, often being referred to as some sort of undefined bad feeling.

A friend has said, "When people write, they are mounting a platform. Who do you want for an audience?" I've had to respond, "My book is not for everybody. But it is for those persons who experience guilt for doing or being less than they feel they ought. It is for those who have, at least secretly, admitted to themselves that they don't like themselves as much as they wished they did. It's for those who are sometimes their own worst enemies – for those who are trying to understand themselves or others – for those who are always doing or saying things that are self-defeating or that cause themselves to be hurt. It is for those who want to see more clearly what the ethical teachings of Jesus really have to do with the work-a-day world and the struggle for survival. It is for pastors who want to better understand their parishioners and for all who counsel troubled souls, whether they couch that service within a setting that is primarily psychological or one that is primarily theological. It is for those who would see what Heaven and Hell have to do with this side of the grave. It is for all who have ever felt as though they were drawn by two forces – one working to tear them down and another working to build him up – one toward light, one toward darkness – one toward life -- one toward death -- one toward Heaven, the other toward Hell. It is for you who have taken the time to read this far.

Guilt feelings generally have taken a "bum rap." Cursed is he who never feels a sense of guilt. Like any other form of pain, guilt feelings tell us that something is wrong. Something needs to be corrected. We are going to be looking at healthy and unhealthy ways of dealing with guilt feelings or the lack of them when they are the appropriate response to some behaviors. As a student of both theology and psychology for more than fifty years, I have drawn many conclusions. One of the most important: people who tend to be cursed by their sense of guilt, also may be blessed by forgiveness.

Many years ago, when Dr. Karl Menninger wrote the book, *Whatever Became of Sin?*, he might well have followed it with Whatever Became Of Guilt? Indeed "sin" and "guilt" are "out of style," but we of the modern era still reap what we've sown, and all too often, we reap from what others have sown. As I have listened to the thousands of people who have shared their concerns, it has seemed that guilt in some form, on someone's part, lies beneath almost every unresolved hurtful experience that is turned over and examined. The older it has become the more rotten and destructive it has become.

Yet, we still don't like to use the word, "guilt." We seem so intimidated by the word and its association with the "old" and the "religious" that we have assigned it to a place in the archives. Instead of talking about "guilt," it is more popular to talk about "low self-esteem," a "bad self-image," of "not O.K.ness," or of "ethical violations," but not of sin and its guilt. If you want to sound philosophical, you may call it "existential estrangement," while your sophisticated friend calls it "un-authenticity." Call it what you will, but to borrow from a warn phrase, "a thorn by any other name is still a thorn," and there is no rose on its stem!

Somewhat like the word "sin," the word "guilt" has something of a theological ring that makes people want to deal with it in other terms – if they deal with it at all. With few exceptions, the word "sin" has been left for use by the poorly educated, screaming, wild-eyed, back-woods preacher who often has more Gospel (good news) in his sermons than those who fill the pulpits of the large city First Churches. You will have to look hard to find either "sin" or "guilt" in contemporary theological writing. Both words are almost totally missing from there also. A cursory survey of a multi-book series, Makers of the Modern Theological Mind, representing the basic contributions of major theologians of the past 150 years, shows a near-total absence of the words. (And all the while, religious leaders across the U.S. seem not to understand why the modern pulpit is accused of being irrelevant.)

By whatever words the Christian community may choose to describe this phenomenon of human experience, when a person says "I feel guilty," just about everybody knows the feeling that he or she is talking about. Most people know that familiar, haunting voice of the "ghost in the closet" who rattles chains of enslavement, binding them to the past. Sigmund Freud was convinced that "the sense of guilt is the most important problem in the development of civilization" (Freud, 1961, p.81). I am convinced that no matter what name it goes under, it is indeed one of the most important problems of humankind today.

Guilt may well be the most universal of all human conflicts. When we have violated our own internally accepted "law", we are haunted by guilt, pursued by guilt, pressed by guilt, depressed by guilt, angered by guilt, weakened by guilt, sickened by guilt, and we *can* be destroyed by guilt.

Acknowledgments

When a book represents the culmination of what a man considers some of his most important thoughts in seventy-seven years of living, it is impossible to acknowledge all those persons whose ideas have influenced his conclusions. To accurately acknowledge, I would have to begin with my parents and continue by naming all my friends, acquaintances, teachers, and all others at all levels of my continuing process of learning.

I would have to name those thousands of patients who chose to share their struggles with me during the thirty-one years that I ministered at their bedside as a professional hospital chaplain. I would have to name the hundreds of students who studied under my supervision when I taught off-campus extension courses and on-campus studies to candidates for Bachelor's, Master's, and Doctoral degrees for twelve colleges, universities, theological seminaries, and graduate schools. I would have to name hundreds of authors after whom I have read across the years.

One group deserves my deepest sense of gratitude: my counselees. I have asked many of them for permission to tell some part of their story. Not one has ever denied me the privilege of quoting him or her when I have promised to hide all personal identity.

Harley Dixon, a retired professional bedside hospital chaplain, counselor, and dear friend of almost fifty years, Deborah Flanagan, a blossoming writer and member of our Heart of the Valley Writers Guild, Dr. Jonathan Zayas, a medical psychotherapist, and Dr. Eunice Reynolds,

Dean of Oxford Graduate School and cherished friend, all gave worthy counsel for manuscript preparation.

Only God is due more gratitude than Ann, my wife of fifty-four years who died while proof-reading the final draft of the manuscript. She listened to my thoughts, encouraged my perseverance, and loved me enough to hide whatever boredom she may have felt at times as she served as a sounding-board and challenger to my thoughts.

While many people have offered worthy counsel during the development of the thoughts herein, I must confess that I have not heeded all of their suggestions. It is I who must take the rostrum. It is I who stand responsible.

William G. Justice
Knoxville, TN

Chapter 1

We Live Under Law

"Damn you! I'll never forgive you for that! I'll make you pay for what you did if it's the last thing I ever do! Killing's too good for you. I'd rather see you suffer! Damn you! Damn you!" His burning eyes saw only himself in the mirror.

I once asked a new counselee if she had ever cursed herself. She looked surprised, "A little voice has been whispering to me all day, 'Damn you! Damn you! Damn you!'"

These two persons may seem to be extreme instances of self-hatred. Perhaps you've never been aware of self-dislike as a problem of your own. But you have seen people do things that harmed themselves when they "knew better." No pleading or logic could persuade them from their own process of self-destructive, self-defeating behavior. You have seen those who are "hell-bent for destruction." You may even suspect that all of us have at least some tendency toward doing things that work against our own best interests.

How do we ever get to the point of disliking or even hating ourselves? How do we ever get enslaved to behavior that clearly defeats our own best interests? Can we ever be free? Yes, but no person is totally free. We are limited by laws. Some were formed by God and are seen in what we call "nature." (You are "free" to leap from a high building, but gravity and a hard surface will make you pay for your foolish act.) Some laws are formally legislated by the state in an effort to keep order and to protect the people. Some were legislated by tradition, social custom, and other sources of authority, with "you ought to" carrying the weight of a law that says, "You must." Violations of the law always carry some threat of penalty. We meet law in some form quite early in life.

"Oughts" Begin in the Womb

Only the womb gave us a period free from the "urge of the ought." Those first "you oughts" were vague, distant, and almost lost, but they had their influence. If memory permitted, the beginning period of life might have been remembered somewhat like this.

The first nine months (those in the womb) were probably the nearest we ever came to being absolutely free. The quarters were somewhat cramped, but we could roll over in "bed" now and then, and kick and move our arms. We were warm, well fed, comfortably sheltered, and aware of absolutely no expectations for doing or not doing a thing. We had no urge that suggested that we ought to act or ought to think in any fashion. We had no sense of responsibility to fulfill anybody's "ought" – not even our own. We were free!

We had been growing fast and many changes were taking place. By kicking and squirming, we became somewhat lodged in a head-down position. Our hearing had developed well enough to hear the pounding of mama's heart and the gurgling noise in her digestive system. Sometimes, that got downright noisy. We were accustomed to the pressures of such tight quarters and the occasional squeeze when mama tried to roll over on her tummy while she slept. But that pressure was nothing compared to the pressures we experienced during the process of labor. The birth process began when the muscles of mama's womb started to contract. That may have been our first time to feel any "urge of oughtness." It was as though we were getting the vague message, "You ought to get out of here. It's time to go." Let's continue as if it just might have happened to you.

Oughts in Birth

The first muscular contractions of your mother's womb probably began about thirty minutes apart and lasted for less than a minute. They soon became more frequent. Your father headed for the hospital with her when the contractions started coming about four minutes apart. In the delivery room, a physician, a nurse, an anesthetist, and a nurse aid were making last-minute preparations for your grand entry into your new world. Your father, feeling helpless, probably stood nervously in the corner with orders to stay out of the way.

Someone wheeled your mama in, placed her on a delivery table while stripping away any remaining trace of her dignity. Your father eased to her side. She tightened her grip on his hand and held on. The labor contractions were getting harder. The pressure on you was getting tremendous, but it was not quite enough.

The attending physician and the nurse began pressing on the outside of your mama's tummy, trying to help push you out. Another first! Persons other than mama were indicating that you "ought" to be somewhere else. And they had the power to enforce their opinion. They applied more pressure. When you barely had your head out into your new world the doctor probably wiped your face. Those actions were saying that you ought not to have that mucous-like fluid all over your face. Then someone stuck the tip of a rubber bulb-suction gadget up each nostril of your nose and drew out the fluids. Using the same gadget, an assistant quickly cleared your mouth and throat. Obviously, they were convinced that you should not have it there any longer. It would have been in the way of your breathing a few moments later.

As if all of that squeezing was not enough discomfort, about that time the doctor may have grabbed your head and given it a twist. Of course, he had seen that you ought to be in a different position for better passage. When the next contraction pushed you forward, the doctor might have thought you ought to hurry out, so he gave you a firm tug. If he talked while he worked, he might have added, "Come on out of there, little fellow." Not even fully out of the womb and there was somebody muttering an "ought" to you and emphasizing it with force. That last tug worked. Out slipped your shoulders, arms, and chest.

As soon as the pressure was off, your lungs expanded and you drew in that first breath of air. If you gurgled a bit, the doctor slapped you briskly on the back. "Ouch!" Now they expected you to breathe! Your own lungs were expected to take in oxygen that mama had formerly supplied. This was your first act of independence. You may have struggled, but you were doing what they expected. "Hey, little one, you are doing fine," whispered a gentle voice. You were doing what you ought. Somebody gave you approval. If you had been able to talk, you might have said, "Grab a blanket and wrap me up. It's cold out here."

About that time, the doctor flipped you on your back and laid you on mama's tummy. That was about as good a table as any. The doctor clamped off the umbilical cord. It was as if he were saying, "You ought to stop being so dependent on your mama's food for your food, and you ought to use another method of getting rid of body waste. You ought to be free of this thing. Snip! There was no going back now.

You had goo all over you. An attending nurse grabbed you and began wiping you dry. That meant that you ought not to have that mucous-like matter all over your body any longer. To get any remaining fluids out of your lungs, she may have laid you in a little heated bed raised at the foot. Then she may have run a tiny tube into your lungs and suctioned out some fluids with an electric pump. That did not feel good, but you could do nothing about it.

Somebody had decided that you ought to be clearly identified, so the nurse put a name-band around your little wrist and took your footprint for permanent record. Knowing that you ought to have your eyes protected from possible infection, she put in drops of antibacterial drugs. To keep you warm on the way to the nursery, the nurse finally wrapped a blanket around you. All of these had been entirely "pre-parental oughts."

Let's pause a few moments and look at the first of a series of line illustrations. (See figure 1.) This earliest developmental period can be shown as a straight line beginning at a dot representing the beginning of human life. The arrow at the end of the solid line represents the "now" point of the beginning pilgrimage. The short span to the left of the arrow point represents the brief past, and all to the right represents the highest potential for the future.

Figure 1

Beginnings

LIFE
at its
highest
potential

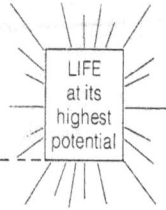

The direction of movement is toward life and its abundance, with the fullest of joy, vitality, fulfillment, realization, contentment, maturity, zest, and satisfaction. The direction is toward the ideal life and the potential that lies within us as a supreme possibility. Direction is toward one's potential. At this early stage of development we are right on course, un-diverted, unburdened, and unhindered. Ideally, relationships for the loved child are in accord during this early period. A harmonious tie of love binds child and parent.

However, the only love for the child that is sure is the love of God. From the moment of conception, every influence by God upon the child is His effort to promote the child's growth toward life's highest potential. Other persons may or may not love the child, and since God's love is most fully expressed through people, the child is blessed who has loving parents – parents who provide, not only affection, but who also habitually work in the child's best interests. All who enter the child's world without love will tend to divert the child from his or her highest potential – from God's intended destination for the child. Awareness of the relationships comes only with time and experience. The child may never fully realize the influence of those relationships on its development.

Figure 2 shows the three dimensions of relationships – relationship with other people, relationship with self, and relationship with God. You will note that in this earliest period of life, *all love is directed toward the child.* Ideally, the child's capacity for wholesome love for God, others, and self will grow as the child grows toward its highest potential.

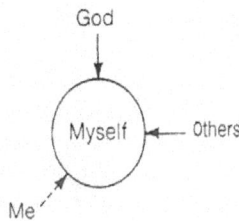

Oughts in "Eden"

When taken to its mother, the tiny infant may run into another "ought" rather abruptly. He "ought" only to suck the nipple of mother's breast. His reward is the flow of warm, satisfying milk. Then, too, he ought not bite her nipple. Violation may bring a frightening "ouch!" and punishment by withdrawal of the breast. Of course, neither reward nor punishment is in the thoughts of either mother or child. (Such simple, ordinary experiences, however, are the early seeds of the awareness that obedience to an "ought" brings reward and disobedience to an "ought" brings punishment.)

The withdrawal of the breast also may be interpreted by the infant as withdrawal of love. This sort of interpretation seems to be the origin of the feeling, "If I do not live up to expectations of others, they will not love me." Such possibilities for the future cultivate early feelings of anxiety. People often speak of the sleeping child as the picture of untroubled innocence. "He looks so relaxed and peaceful." He has no willful violation of any "ought" to trouble his mind. Anxiety is yet to be developed, and he bears no sense of guilt.

He is, however, aware of approval and disapproval – of acceptance and rejection. All the while he is getting a steady flow of "oughts" from those people on whom he has to depend. He ought to take milk, be clean, sleep at night, and refrain from crying.

These earliest "oughts" all become a part of those to be sifted later for selection and blended into a system of "internalized" rule by law.

The early "oughts" are admittedly small in proportion to the ocean of "oughts" experienced during a normal life span. They are, however, at least comparable to the tiny droplet of dew that falls from a leaf high on a mountain and slowly makes its way to become part of the sea. Though small, these early experiences are a part of the sense of obligation that grows daily with the child.

In I'm OK – You're OK, Thomas Harris' highly popular book of the 1960s, Harris gave an excellent condensation of a study by Dr. Wilder Penfield. Penfield's research supports the theory that all of the sights, sounds, odors, tastes, and feelings of every experience are all recorded and stored within the cells of the brain. The material in this vast memory bank is recorded "stereophonically," as if dual tracks were set into the brain, with the memory recorded on one track and the associated feelings related to the memory recorded on the other. At a later time, the memory and the feelings may be brought back together, or they may possibly return separately, one without the other. Either or both may be "forgotten." The memory may return without the "forgotten" associated feelings or the feelings may return without the "forgotten" associated memory. This "forgotten" matter is "repressed." Of course, only a relatively small portion of our past can be recalled at will. The remainder stays submerged in a growing, ever-changing, restless collection of past experiences (Harris, pp.1-15).

The birth experience and those early events of life become lost in this vast sea of impressions and feelings that make up every person's past and help make every person unique.

The smile, the frown, the irritated tone of voice, and everything else is recorded within, and to each there is a personal response. In this set of recordings are the thousands of "no's" directed at the toddler and the repeated "don'ts" that have bombarded him while the parents try to prepare the child for life in his or her corner of civilization. Recorded are the looks of embarrassment and horror in its mother's face when his curiosity brought shame on the family in the form of nail polish poured out on the neighbor's carpet. (When we consider the thousands of no's a small child hears, it is no wonder that many small children go through a period when they respond "no" to almost everything said to them.)

It is easy for the small child to conclude that there is little he can do that is correct in the eyes of the "big people," who may seem to be as gods. It is later that the "law" is more clearly put into words and imposed upon the child. "It's a sin to waste food." "Don't pick your nose." "Cleanliness is next to Godliness." "Always respect your elders." "Idleness is the devil's workshop." "You must always keep your pants on in public." "Never eat with your elbows on the table." The child's "oughts" come by the dozens. The original Adam seems to have had only one forbidden fruit, but his descendants have many. Most commandments come from the ultimate authority figure in the life of the child – the parent. Those giants are the source of security, and they must be pleased and obeyed.

But they aren't the only ones who make known what behavior is expected and what gains approval or disapproval. Brothers and sisters, aunts and uncles, parents of playmates and of course the playmates themselves all express their own approval or disapproval. Indeed, the entire culture in which the small child is developing tells him what he should and should not do. Almost everyone is saying by word or attitude, "You ought to. . ." Also by word, action, or attitude each provides a punishment (disapproval) or a reward (approval).

Another voice that must be taken into account is that of God. Though the concept of "God" seems yet to be formed in the child's mind, we have to consider this also as a possible early source of instruction.

Some have suggested that God gives prerecorded instructions to the child at the moment of conception – by DNA? Does He teach some universal "rights' and "wrongs" while the child is yet in the womb? Does He engrave them into the child's spirit during infancy? Regardless of the time, there is little in the young child's behavior to show that he or she responds positively to any possible divine voice of leadership. Adam and Eve rebelled against instruction soon after their creation. The small child wastes little time before following in the steps of those primal parents.

We are uncomfortably aware of the cruelty of children. A child with a crossed eye may be treated as savagely by his peers as they may treat a grasshopper. Without the slightest twinge of remorse, and with equal glee, they can jeer "goofy eyes" or pull the legs off a grasshopper. Both the cross-eyed child and the grasshopper are assumed to exist for children's amusement.

Such behavior and attitudes have forced many authorities to agree with those of the previous century: "the child has no innate intuition of what is right or wrong, nor the innate ideas of moral quality of emotions, thoughts, or behavior" (Mairet, 1956. p.34). We are forced to conclude that if any sense of "oughtness" is given early by God, any evidence of its presence lies dormant for the first few years.

Oughts in Nature

One additional voice of law comes from nature. Just as the small child has no detectable concept of God, the child has no concept of physics. Laws of heat, gravity, friction, and momentum are less than meaningless. Of course, it is the responsibility of the parents to warn of the dangers in violating the laws set by nature. Even the three-year-old has begun to learn the dangers that exist in his world and will warn the younger child. What the parents or others do not say, nature will say for itself. It will speak loudly and clearly. But it teaches cruelly.

Natural laws speak by way of the toy saying, "Don't stand up in the wagon." From the open fireplace and the top of the kitchen stove it says, "Don't touch hot things." Nature's laws have built-in penalties, and ignorance of the laws is no excuse. The consequences are the same to the enlightened and to the ignorant. Reward comes in obedience, and punishment is the natural consequence of disobedience. The small child who pulls the pot of boiling soup from the stove experiences the entire process of "arrest, trial, conviction, and punishment" that is all carried out in one sickening moment of encounter between scalding fluid and tender flesh.

Fortunately, the consequences are not always this severe. A bump, scratch, or smarting finger is more typical of the penalty, but the child begins to get the idea, "I'm free to do as I please within certain limits. I can seemingly cross some limits without apparent injury (from nature or parents), but if I cross other limits, I will experience painful results. How am I going to deal with those limits?" He will live within the limits or he will endure the consequences. He will obey or he will suffer.

Ought Becomes Law

It is for this reason that law must be clearly taught. Parents live with the moral duty to warn of dangerous circumstances or objects in the child's world that would injure him or would entice him to injure himself. Not only must limits be taught, but love requires them to be enforced. The child who does not find his limitations or behavior enforced may conclude that he is not loved.

A friend overheard her daughter and another child at play. The children were sitting on the ground beneath an open window while the mother cleaned house. The visiting child said, "My mama and daddy let me do anything I want to." After a brief pause, my friend's child responded, "Gee, your mama and daddy must not love you very much if they let you do anything you want to." When my own son David was about seven or eight, he told me the same thing, "Daddy, if you let me do things that you know would hurt me, I'd think you didn't love me."

These are typical conclusions. Several of my counselees have told me that they grew up feeling unloved because their parents set few or no limits. Children who have been told by parents or others, "Don't touch hot things," may respond with obedience or they may choose to respond by defiance. They may be not yet experienced or knowledgeable enough to know that their parent's demands are for the children's benefit. The parents are not being capricious. They are telling the child to keep hands off hot things because they know from experience that the child is going to be harmed if he grabs something hot. Whether they tell him or not, the consequences are the same. Whether he believes them or not, the consequences are the same. Each demand becomes a sort of law.

Much of this came into focus for me many years ago after a rather normal vacation experience. Having arrived at a mountain retreat, Ann and I started to unload the car. Our children Lisa and David, ages eight and five, had begun to explore their new surroundings. I suddenly remembered that the area is well known for its sandstone gorges with sheer cliffs – some with drops of a hundred feet or more. I decided to do some exploring of my own.

Both children came running when I stepped to the porch and called. With a child holding each hand, we began our stroll. I was watching for broken glass or anything else in the area on which the children might hurt themselves. At the back corner of the cabin, I spotted the most beautiful, lush, green patch of poison ivy that I had ever seen. It could not have been prettier if it had been under cultivation. In fact, the caretaker had carefully mowed around it. Knowing that the children were familiar with the harmless ivy growing in our yard at home, I realized that they needed to be warned. We squatted down to talk about it.

"Lisa and David, this is poison ivy. It's something you must not touch. You could pull off the leaves of this poison ivy right now and rub it on your hands or wipe it on your face. If you did, you would not be aware of any harm from it until tomorrow morning when your skin would turn red and start to itch. Within a few hours, little red pimples would begin to form that would fill with something like water, and the whole lot would itch like crazy everywhere you have touched it to your skin. Please stay away from it."

Having circled the cabin and looked over the rest of the area, I started back inside to help Ann get everything organized for our stay. From the porch, I called back "Lisa and David, we are going to be here for several days. We're here to have fun. Play in the yard anywhere you want except at the back corner of the cabin. Please stay away from the poison ivy."

They expressed faith in me and believed that I was concerned for their best interests by obeying me. Weeks passed before I noticed several parallels between this incident and the experience in the Garden of Eden recorded in the second and third chapters of Genesis in the Old Testament. One is worthy of reflection here.

Why did I establish a behavioral law? "Thou shalt not touch." A law involving physics and the plant's chemistry was already in force. Touching would have caused harm. The child may view the law as unreasonable or capricious. My statement was being expressed as a law during the period of life when the child was lacking in adequate knowledge. The child cannot know, by previous experience, the consequence of violating the law of chemistry and physics. Love requires that the one in the role of parent must put warnings into words.

The child grows best within a climate of love. Loved, he learns to love. Feeling loved by those in the parent role, he is more inclined to feel loved by God, and even worthy of loving himself. Parent's attitude toward him will usually determine the attitude he feels he deserves to hold for himself. He also tends to give back that love in all directions. (See figure 3.) It is important to recognize that we have the capacity to project ourselves outside ourselves and to relate to that self in an interpersonal relationship.

Figure 3

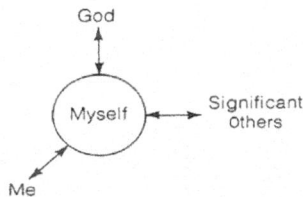

In addition to the observable laws of physics are other laws that relate to interpersonal behavior. By their very nature, they are less readily observable. Therefore, some people doubt that they exist.

The laws related to electricity are not suspended in behalf of the unwise child who sticks bobby pins into the wall outlet. Neither are the laws related to human behavior suspended as a child secretly hates his baby sister, or as he lies about having pulled the knob off the dish washer, or as he angrily chokes and kills the family pet. He is inwardly harmed – eroded by each. The cause-and-effect laws related to human attitude and behavior are just as real and reliable as the consequences involving the violation of physical laws.

Parents are responsible to make the child aware of the natural laws of the world of physics. It is also their responsibility to make the child aware of the natural laws of the world of human attitude and behavior. Obedience to the laws produces reward and disobedience of the laws results in harm.

Figure 4

A Modern Child's "Garden"
The law by which we fail to live
will be the law by which we will tend to die.

It will be necessary to return to this concept for a more thorough development within another context. It should suffice for now to assert that it is important for every child to learn that he lives under law. And violation of the law brings harm that is inclined toward death. The law by which we fail to live will be the law by which we will tend to die. (See figure 4.)

"Right and Wrong" "Constructive and Destructive"

Though we have considered the earliest materials that go into the development of the sense of "oughtness," I have avoided the words, "right" and "wrong," "moral" and "immoral," nor have any value judgments been made in reference to "good" or "evil." Because of the many biases and pre-conditioned responses of these words that have led to misunderstandings, they are generally avoided throughout this book. For reasons that I hope to make increasingly obvious, instead of the usual evaluative words such as "good" and "bad," I prefer to use "constructive" and "destructive," "helpful" and "harmful," or "healing" and "sickening."

For the sake of clarity and for my own sense of integrity, it seems best now to state that the material of this text is presented on the premise that "good," "moral," or "right" is that which is constructive – that which makes a positive contribution toward self-acceptance, fullness, richness, and abundance of life for one's neighbor and for one's self. That which is "bad," "evil," "immoral," or "wrong" is that which erodes, degenerates, or in any way contributes to the destruction of the potential for experiencing life's highest good for one's neighbor and for one's self.

Chapter 2

We are Legislators

Up to this point, we have been focusing mainly on the pre-conscience period of development – the period of growth in which other people's values, other people's laws or code of morality have been imposed upon us. All "oughts" have been "you ought." The directing voice has been external. But we can't spend life with a parent or friend or preacher or policeman telling us what we "ought" or "ought not" to do in every instance. We cannot be as the little wooden boy, Pinocchio, with a Jiminy Cricket to shout when we are about to do the wrong thing or go in the wrong direction. To depend solely on an outside voice would leave us immature. Maturity demands that the primary controlling voice must be inside us.

The Election to Office of Legislator

As we become more mature, self-government becomes more and more important. Each person feels he has to establish his own code of behavior – his own set of binding moral principles. This sense of self-direction is necessary if he is to "grow up." The sense of self-command is part of the formation of his individuality as a person.

Taking rule of his own life, he elects himself as his own legislator with the right and responsibility to hear opinions of others and to examine their behavior codes. But the judgment of others is no longer adequate. Each person wants and needs his own approval and disapproval of what "ought" and "ought not" to be.

We Hear the Lobbyists

All who influence those decisions are comparable to lobbyists. Of course, from the very beginning it is the parent's words, actions, and attitudes that are of prime importance. With minor changes, most of us confirm the code of our parents. If they smoke, we will be inclined to smoke. If they gossip, we will be inclined to gossip. Our inner code of behavior will bear the evidence of our heritage and the influence of our culture and immediate environment. All lobbyists urge for approval of their own value system of behavior. "Adopt this as a statute into your code of law. Make it a part of your internal guidance system – your value system – your ethical standard." They persuade, "speak kindly to old folks. Don't masturbate. Don't throw trash along the roadside." Their instructions seem endless.

The voices have given repeated warnings with the instructions. But eventually, through our own choice, they become our own voice, in such a way that we cannot distinguish between the various sources. The conscience is forming with its stored concepts of value and good behavior. The voices are becoming so blended and internalized that they are becoming our own voice.

Each lobbyist exercises powers of persuasion with logic and emotion If there are those who are against the adoption of an act into law, they also are heard: "There's nothing wrong with cheating on a test." Both rational thoughts and feelings affect the debate within the self in the making of laws for a personal code of ethics. The self in the role of legislator acts and decides, "I will never steal even a pencil." "I will never cheat on a test in school." "I will always be kind to animals." The developing child makes independent decisions, repeatedly saying in essence,

"Here I stand." With each "stand," another decision is adopted and written into the inner ethical code-book. Of all the lobbyists, the role of the parents remains most important during the period in which the child is rapidly adopting one bill of legislation after another. Every child has looked to his parents and has heard them express, by word or by action, "This is the way you ought to be." The child's typical response is, "But I want to do what I want to do when I want to do it."

James Knight has described the process: He will relinquish this pleasurable but disapproved behavior in return for . . . loving parental acceptance. The child is weak and helpless. His parents are big and strong. He uses the politician's dictum, "If you can't lick them, join them!". . . . He joins them, and makes their ways and wishes his ways. This is the beginning of incorporation and identification. In this early stage, he is adopting certain patterns of behavior which emanate from persons and standards unto himself as his own value system, and thus, his true conscience is developed.

Knight goes on to remind us that the child further takes as his own the moral standards of heroes about whom he reads and of important figures in his community, such as his teachers and his minister (Knight, p.11). These decisions are also influenced by the behavior of persons of renown such as political figures and entertainers. I listened recently to a teen-age girl. She said that since former president Bill Clinton had indulged in oral sex, she had decided that oral sex on dates with boys was OK.

Formation of a Concept of God

We cannot say precisely how early a concept of "God" begins, but mounting evidence suggests that it begins soon after birth, long before any religious training. It is the parent who speaks the voice of authority to which the child may credit some divine authority.

Ancient Jewish tradition required the parents to choose the spouse for their child. They assumed that the parent's spiritual maturity opened them to the leadership of God to which the developing child did not have access. The parent was believed to speak for God.

If the modern child does not credit the parents with speaking for the divine, the parents are likely to claim divine knowledge for themselves. Paul Tournier, for nearly fifty years one of the most respected Medical Doctors in Geneva, asserted that this practice is universal.

All men claim to express, through their own judgments, the judgment of God Himself....Men make a monopoly of God, even those who do not believe in Him . . . they judge the conduct of others, . . . A child cannot receive his first lessons in morality directly from God; he receives them from his parents. . . . There are indeed genuine divine truths which parents thus hand on to their children -- for instance, that in general, lying is culpable (Tournier, p.72).

All wisdom, food and clothing, and knowledge have seemingly centered in the parents. Though the mother seems all-sufficient in the provision of food and the child has been biologically dependent on her, it is the father who seems all-powerful. And, being male, he is seen as most representative of God. For a time, the father may be not merely representative of God, he may seem to *be* God.

My own sociological research and that of several others suggests that the small child looks to the parents and somewhere along the way concludes that God has identical personality characteristics as his or her parents – identifying the characteristics of God primarily with the father (Justice, 1984). Many parents are uncomfortable with the idea that their children are looking at them and concluding that, "God is just like my daddy (or mother)." Since the evidence suggests that children are inclined to carry this belief into adulthood, and throughout their lives, we parents face a heavy responsibility that has temporal and eternal implications.

The father usually is the strongest person in the small child's tiny world. Of course, when there is no father in the home, the child must look to the father of friends and acquaintances for the meaning of the concept of "father." The experience of listening in the counseling office forces many of us to concur with Sigmund Freud, J.B. Phillips, and Edward Stein who said, "Religion is . . . a projection onto the cosmos of family structure, that God is projected as father (psychologically), and that this basis of trust is the sustaining, biding meaning that makes religion crucial to man" (Stein, p.193). Phillips adds, "The early conception of God is almost invariably founded upon the child's idea of his father (p.19). Does this, then, explain away God?

Some insecure religious people get uncomfortable in the presence of such ideas. And the irreligious may use such statements to fortify an atheistic stance. But listen to more of what Stein has to say. "It is perfectly possible that the way which the Intelligent Power who is the Ground of Being, made Himself known, revealed Himself, was by making man biologically dependent upon parents and prone to such projection." Psychological explanation does not account for religious truth. It may, however, throw light on it.

I have long suspected that Freud's argument against religion could be applied in reverse -- that his negative feelings related to his own weak father stimulated him to want to eliminate a cosmic Father. Recall that we have mounting evidence to support the theory that humans commonly look to their own fathers and conclude that "God is just like my daddy." The concept of "father" can have as many negative connotations as positive – often more.

The growing awareness of that fact was the primary motive for me to enroll in a second graduate school and for the research that I reported in my doctoral dissertation (Justice, 1984). I began hearing statements that indicated a misunderstanding of the nature of God because of the nature of several counselees' fathers. The day before originally writing the thoughts on this page, a counselee said, "I grew up with my idea of what the word *father* meant. When I heard God called the Father, how else could I think of God than as my own father? When my father was cold and distant, it was just a few meaningless words to hear God called 'loving',"

Another person recently said that because her father was harsh in his judgment, as well as stern and unforgiving of her, it was hard to expect that God as the Father could ever be accepting and forgiving. "It seems that God expects me to be perfect before he will accept me, just like my father." (The Christian concept of grace, God's unearned, unmerited, favor of any kind seemed difficult for her mind to grasp.) That last phrase of her statement reminds me of similar words that were opposite in their overall effect.

I overheard a conversation between a six year-old and her aunt.

"Honey; where do you think God is?"
"Real close to me."
"How close?"
"So close that sometimes I can almost feel His whiskers just like my Daddy's."

Parents have the awesome responsibility to communicate the love, patience, and leadership that will make possible a healthy transfer of trust, and devotion to the true eternal God.

These things have been said within the larger subject of the development of the conscience. The conscience is that which enables us to compare our behavior "to that inner codebook, judging good and evil, reproaching when we have done wrong and granting a sense of peace when we have done well. Webster says, "Conscience is a power to decide the moral quality of one's own thoughts or acts."

Dangerous Assumptions

Many declare the conscience to be the voice of God. Granting that God may use the conscience as a guide to behavior, we must, however, remember that in the development of conscience, many resources have been used and not all are constructive to one's self or others. It can be easily perverted and morbidly developed by the extremely sensitive person and ignored or silenced by the insensitive.

Recently, I listened as a man expressed how his conscience "bothered" him for shooting a sitting bird. He had been taught from childhood that to shoot a bird in flight was OK, but to shoot it while sitting was "wrong."(I could not comfortably shoot a dove because of my own early trainings.)

The conscience may lead one person to act in ways usually considered "wrong," whereas the conscience may keep another from doing that which is usually considered "right." Every mental-health worker knows of those who have stolen, cheated, raped, and murdered while following the direction of some inner voice they identified as "God" or the "conscience." Earlier in the week before writing these lines, reporters were describing a man who strangled his small child because, "God told me to do it."

Most people consider it the "right" thing to do, to enter a place of worship. Yet a Protestant may feel the pangs of a distressed conscience by attending a Roman Catholic Mass, and the Roman Catholic may experience the same degree of distress if he or she attends a Protestant service of worship.

Wanda told of a conflict growing out of early teachings forbidding the entry to *any* place of worship. "It seems as if every time we drove by a church, mama would say something like, 'Don't you ever go into one of those places. People who go there are evil. They are hypocrites. They are pretending to be good. They are pretending to be God's people but they are evil and corrupt. I'd rather see you dead or in a house of prostitution than ever to know of you going into a church.'" When in her teens, she violated this "ought" by attending a worship service in a church nearby. "I felt dirty and immoral by just being there."

In Walt Disney's old movie version of Pinocchio, I believe it was Jiminy Cricket who sang the refrain, "... always let your conscience be your guide." Though it was a delightful little song for children, we must challenge its wisdom. We must challenge the conscience also. It is not to be trusted without intelligent questioning and close scrutiny – comparing it to such external standards as the Ten Commandments and the moral/ethical teachings of Jesus.

Tyranny of the Ought

As the conscience grows, it is slowly granted more and more rule. The blossoming personality becomes somewhat proud of its evolving code of behavior and its force of inner rule. Ever so slowly the inner sense of "oughtness" gains strength, rewarding for "good" behavior and punishing for behavior labeled "bad." A large percentage of developing persons have failed to notice that this useful and valuable aid to constructive behavior was growing into a Frankenstein monster with the most terrible destructive powers. Like a Rip Van Winkle, one may awaken one day to find there has been a *coup d' etat* -- a take-over -- a revolutionary change. The "ought" has taken command. It has become a dictator -- a merciless despot. Reason, having been dethroned, is permitted only a puppet-rule over behavior. The victim may strive to act as he "ought", but not necessarily in the way that is best.

Few masters are more savage, more oppressive than former slaves. The unleashed conscience is no exception. Its laws become exact in detail and petty in nature, carrying mandatory, severe penalties. Still further, in telling one what to do, the more tyrannical sense of "ought" will insist upon the adoption of almost every requirement that anyone suggests. I will always clean my plate. I must not make anyone angry. I must not enjoy sexual intercourse. Early signs of fragmentation develop with the rupture between reason and conscience. What seems best and right for the developing person is becoming harmful. Overly demanding of one's self, he fails! He is unable – inadequate to live up to all of the demands of conscience. Failure may become a part of his identity. He is a failure. *He* is inadequate. If someone asked behind closed doors, in an unthreatening atmosphere, "Who are you?" he could easily answer, "I am a failure." Unhealthy? Yes. Evidence of insecurity? Yes. Destined for misery? Yes. Evidence of a desperate longing for acceptance? Yes.

But risking overstatement, I assert my own suspicion that we are speaking of an extremely large percentage of the American public. To me, the overly developed sense of "oughtness" explains much of the low self-esteem carried by so many North Americans. To compensate, it is hidden by arrogance and an exaggerated sense of self-worth.

And it grows out of the work of an overly active legislator. (We'll return to other factors related to the sense of worth in the next chapter.) One bill at a time is debated. Should I ever speak angrily to an elder person? Will I ever cheat in school? Debate ends. The one vote is cast. Though the decision is by a majority of one, it is unanimous. If rejected, it can come up for debate at a later time and once again it may be considered for passage. If adopted, it is written as a statue upon the pages of the internal code-book and begins, "henceforth and forever more...." Once adopted, this internalized law has little probability of repeal.

Attempt at repeal typically requires a near-endless debate followed by a rather weak vote. Rarely is the vote decisive. In reference to this sort of conflict, a middle-aged woman said, "I know it sounds silly but, I cannot lay a hat or coat on the bed. I'd like to be free to put a piece of clothing where I want to, but I must have heard mama say a thousand times over that we should never put a hat or coat on the bed. It was so emphatic that it seemed to have had a moral connotation. I decided that mama was right and we would never put hats or coats on the bed. After all these years I finally asked mama about it a few months ago. She didn't know and asked her mother who was more than ninety years old. She said they used to be afraid of infesting the bed with lice or "bed-bugs" and had simply made it a practice to never place on the bed hats or coats of those who came to visit. Now I know that it was simply a practical rule that our family has passed from generation to generation. But I still can't do it. My mind says that there is nothing immoral or wrong about putting hats or coats on the bed, but when I do it you wouldn't believe how guilty I feel."

The permanent recording of the voice and attitude of her mother combined with the recording of her own decision, "I will never. . . ," makes highly unlikely any repeal of that internalized law. Far more than logic went into the forming of that law, and far more than logic would be required for repeal.

The analogy we may use to describe own legal code will largely determine our reaction to having violated it. Do we see our inner code of law as a whole, corporate "set", or as a collection of separate rules?

The difference is important. If we have formed our "Law" as a corporate body, a "set", we will respond differently to violations than if we formed them as separate parts of a "collection." In our travels, my wife and I picked up a demitasse set of fine Bavarian china. If only one of those little cups gets broken, the set will be broken. Since many people form their internal law as a set or collective unit, when any point of their inner law is broken, the "set" is broken (violated).

Others form their internal law as a collection somewhat comparable to eggs in a basket. When one is broken, only the separate one among others is damaged. The violation (breaking) of one is viewed as of little consequence as compared to the whole collection. Which is "better"? Since that is a part of our personality we are not likely to change, we will leave that for the philosophers to debate. But some certainly will be broken.

Chapter 3

We Are Condemned Already

Condemned by the New World

There is no way for a child to live without some sense of condemnation. We came into the world in a flare of violence called birth. From warmth, darkness, and security, we were thrust into a cold room, flooded with brilliant light and loud voices. During birth the child is usually roughly handled and otherwise treated as a "thing," as he is squeezed, pulled, twisted and struck. He is attacked – assaulted while being birthed.

Some researchers have collected evidence that strongly suggests that the first ten minutes after birth are among the most feeling-filled moments in a person's life, leaving permanent marks upon the personality. How can one feel welcomed and accepted when upon arrival into his new world he is greeted by hostility?

Is it possible that the newly born child vaguely feels, "What's wrong? Am I judged unfit to come into your world?" No matter how gentle or how violent his birth, he soon realizes that he is small. Therefore he is inferior in size. He is lacking knowledge. He is lacking in ability to do as he sees adults do and he is, therefore, truly inadequate. He fails to be as others around him. All of this, he feels as a condemnation upon himself. His mere existence seems to judge him as he slowly grows. The pain experienced by others may cause him to condemn himself. If, while preparing her young child's breakfast, hot bacon grease pops on mama's hand, he feels responsible for the pain to this person he loves because she is hurt doing something for him.

While chatting with our daughter, Lisa, she recalled an event that had happened roughly thirty years earlier. One evening I was building a desk and a set of bookshelves for her. It had been entirely my idea. I had recognized that she needed a place to do her schoolwork. She sat on the top bunk of her bed joyfully watching the final assembly. With my last grunt, hefting everything into place against the wall, a shelf slid from its bracket and fell, hitting me on the head. As I looked up, Lisa began to cry. She later explained, "But Daddy, you were doing something for me when you got hurt." She was saying that had it not been for her, I would not have been injured. Had she not existed, I would not have been hurt. She felt responsible, but I was the one actually responsible. The only one who blamed her for my injury was herself. Of course, we are looking at an example of "false guilt." We experience false guilt when we feel guilty when we are not truly guilty. Lisa had done, thought, or felt nothing for which she was responsible, but she felt guilty. We will return to the issue of false guilt within another context.

But I did sometimes judge her behavior. Children cannot live up to the demands of all the "laws" or requirements made by everyone in their world. When they become aware of their failures, they feel rejected and condemned. The child usually responds to criticism by feeling diminished -- cut down -- somewhat less than he previously saw himself. With each critical word, his sense of worth erodes. His action that violated the particular standard of behavior does not get the evaluation. It is he that is evaluated. If his actions are "bad", he is evaluated as a "bad" child. Or if his behavior gets approval, he is a "good" child. Since the child usually hears far more negative than positive, he tends to conclude that he is "bad."

Condemned by Others

Doctors readily insist that the mother's affection (or lack of affection), anxiety, or anger are communicated to the child from the first moments the child is brought to her. Researchers have concluded that the parent's attitudes are "emoted" to the child even weeks before birth. By an "empathic" communication the unborn child feels loved or rejected and tends to carry those feelings even into adulthood. Consider the following statistics: most North American marriages are in trouble. Roughly fifty percent end in divorce.

More than thirty percent of all births in the United States are outside the bonds of marriage. For many years, roughly one bride in five has been pregnant on the day she marries. Although the figures vary slightly from time to time, the point is that a large percentage of children arrive unwanted. And even those who arrived while wanted are often used later as weapons of revenge by couples while fighting, or they are used for some other equally unhealthy purpose. A child is little, but he's not likely to be stupid. My wife, who was a pre-school educator, has said on many occasions, "For the young child, every experience is a learning experience, either a good one or a bad one." Even the very young child senses when something's wrong in his world. Unfortunately, while young and inexperienced, he usually concludes that something is wrong with him.

Questioning whether he was possibly the "cause" of his parents marrying, many a child has rummaged through old family documents secretly looking for a marriage certificate by which he can figure the number of months between the parents' marriage and his birth. If he fears he is the cause of their having married, he is usually feeling he is the cause of any unhappiness he sees between them.

Realistically, almost every child is, at times, the source of some disagreement between parents. Few events within a household place a greater strain on relationships, requiring more adjustments, than the birth of a child. The child often concludes, "If I didn't exist, they would be happy. I'm bad for them." "For them," is usually dropped, resulting in the belief, "I'm bad."

In a divorce procedure, the custody of children is often a part of a heated debate. The children, all too often, conclude that they are really the cause of the whole conflict that is separating the parents. The secret feeling of responsibility and shame may be carried through life -- a life of self-condemnation. Insensitive parents, in the presence of their children, too often, say clearly that their children "weren't planned for," or "We really hoped for a boy. Ha! Ha! Ha!" Comments to imply that all three children were "accidents" aren't at all funny to the children playing on the floor, but quietly listening to a lively chat among parents. The child who concludes, "I wasn't wanted," easily translates this into the feeling into, "I'm not wanted." And, "unwanted' is easily translated into "unloved." Consequently, the child emotionally bleeds, with the feeling, "I am not loved, nor have I ever been loved."

The child, who for any reason feels unloved, usually feels that something is drastically wrong with him. The fact that his parents may lack the capacity for loving usually evades him. He just knows he isn't getting the kind of affection other children seem to get from their parents. The resulting "I'm not O.K." becomes a part of a growing sense of dis-ease.

Blair and Rita Justice, in *The Abusing Family* (p.15) recognize the impossibility of accurately determining the number of children abused each year in the U.S. They do, however, refer to the problem as an epidemic that may constitute the nation's largest single public health problem. Although their work is almost twenty-five years old, those who work with troubled children believe little has changed. They reported several studies suggesting well above 1.5 million cases of child abuse per year and possibly increasing at a rate of 30 percent a year!

The unfortunate child, born to abusive parents, often concludes, "Though I don't know what is so bad about me, I must be getting what I deserve." A woman confided that she could vividly remember beatings that resulted in large bruises and sometimes broken bones. "I can't remember a time I didn't hate mama. Other children seemed to love their mother. I knew I must be evil to have only feelings of hate for mine. It may sound strange, but the only time I remember being happy was after one of her beatings. When she beat me, I felt she was just giving me what I deserved. I hated me as much as I hated her."

As suggested earlier, we may even feel condemned by others or by ourselves for events predating birth. A counselee recalled that the great depression of the 1930's was at its lowest. The shack they called home was cold most of the time throughout the winters. Mr. Jackson knew that the hunger of his wife and six children was seldom relieved. The only thing that seemed abundant was the "want" he saw in his children's tattered rags and his wife's thin, drawn cheeks. They were his responsibility, and he was failing to provide as he felt he ought. The depression for him became both economic and emotional. The gray turned black. Helen tearfully announced that she was pregnant! One more mouth would need to be fed. One more back would need to be clothed. A thousand other responsibilities of parenthood lay on his shoulders. Combined with all other inner conflicts, it was simply more than the man could handle. It was not a rabbit he really intended to kill as he walked out of the house with the 12-gauge shotgun in hand. He killed himself less than two weeks before the birth of his tiny daughter Elaine.

After more than 40 years, Elaine sat tearfully remembering the family plight. She remembered her frail mother's determination to keep the family together. But every want and need of the family was a reminder that all would have been better if she had never been born. Every drop of milk, every morsel of food, and every thread of clothing she had, deprived the others of what they would have had if she had never existed. She loved her brothers and sisters, but as she saw other families with a father in the home, she felt her own family had been robbed of a father because of her. For more than 40 years Elaine had daily reminders that she was responsible for the death of her father and the suffering of her family. She felt condemned by the world and by herself just for being alive. (An amazing coincidence: later in the day, after writing Elaine's story for you, a man looked across my desk and asked, "Have you ever heard of anybody feeling guilty -- just for being alive?") Once again, we are seeing false guilt – feelings of guilt for things over which one has had absolutely no responsibility or control.

Almost every person whose mother died giving birth feels a kinship with Elaine. Though it may never be spoken, the feeling tends to persist, "Because of me, daddy doesn't have a wife and my brothers and sisters no longer have a mother." At low moments, the feeling creeps in, "They are too kind to say it, but they really blame me for mama's death." Of course this kind of projection is really saying, "I blame me for mama's death. I ought never to have been born." Still other sources condemn the small child. Even his or her general physical appearance can be used to produce a sense of rejection and condemnation. We were thinking earlier about the ridicule of the child with a crossed eye. "Fat-so ", "Bones", and "Shorty" are also condemned by nicknames related to their appearance. People with red hair are often criticized for being "hot headed." How, other than by anger, could they respond to a nickname of "Red" that is almost always pinned on early and carried throughout life? Labels tend to condemn by ridicule. They seem always to point to that which is different. And being different can stir feelings of self-condemnation. Since being different is usually equated by the small child with being bad, he feels, "I ought not to be different. I ought not to be bad."

Appearance is almost invariably a factor that determines acceptance or rejection. In a chapter entitled, "Beauty: The Gold Coin of Human Worth," Dr. James Dobson perfectly makes his point that the ugly live under a sense of condemnation (Dobson, p.15). The attractive one is more easily accepted. One's appearance is his label. But even for the very pretty this may work destructively. "I know that inside I'm not as I appear on the outside." Labels usually tell us what to expect to find within. The child inwardly declares, "I ought to live up to the expectations (the labels) placed on me." Good or bad, healthy or unhealthy, he strives to carry them out. It's truly unfortunate when the expectation is low. It will normally contribute to emotional deterioration.

An adage among the mountain people of East Tennessee says, "Give a dog a bad name and he'll kill himself living up to it." Many who have never gone beyond the third grade have learned in the college of experience that people tend to live up to the expectations placed on them by the people important to their well-being. The child tends to vow, "I'll be what you expect me to be. And I'll tend to act in keeping with the labels you pin on me. I *will tend to be as I see me through your eyes.* I ought to live up to my labels."

The irritated parent may scream a caustic accusation at the child, hoping to force a change in behavior. "You mean little devil! You little liar! You little slob!" Instead of changing in the face of such attacks, the child confirms them by becoming almost enslaved by the bonds of his label. He must try to be the little devil. He must lie. He must work to be the little slob.

This is a part of the danger of equating what the child *is* with what he does. He does not have the maturity of judgment to recognize that he is not bad because he knocked over the glass of milk at the table or lied about having broken the lid to the terrarium. They may be called bad acts without evaluating his total personhood. His label, "You are a bad boy" is all-inclusive. He responds, "I stand condemned by those important for my survival. I will tend to think of me as I feel others think of me. They seem to know everything. Since they seem always correct, they are correct now. I am bad."

The child becomes conditioned to seeing himself as "bad." In his eyes, his bad action has made him a bad person. This characteristic has been described as "condition badness," which is registered inwardly as feelings of guilt. Instead of being bad because he has done something wrong, he sees himself as bad because he *is* something wrong! He is small. He is lacking knowledge. He *is* inferior. He is ugly. He is angry. He *is* unwanted. He is not OK. Any of these beliefs typically make him feel that he is bad. He is failing to be as he feels he "ought" to be. But it is more than a feeling. He may feel it's all a part of his basic identity -- "I am guilty!"

Feelings of guilt emerge from any kind of bad identity. Therefore, an inward sense of guilt precedes morality. Guilt becomes a bad identity. "I am bad, or wrong, or angry, or inferior, or unlovable, etc.," all become his identity -- "I am guilty." If he looks different; if he feels that he is not living up to expectations; if he feels a sense of inadequacy or inferiority; if he feels any of these, they are experienced as feelings of guilt (Tournier, p.24). And the child may be yet too young to have done anything "wrong." He has had guilt thrust upon him. His, "guilt" is by imposition; not by intention or action. He bears false guilt. While still truly "innocent" he feels condemned. He feels guilty. And his feelings of condemnation have tended truly to condemn him. They have diverted him from the most constructive, beneficial, healthy route of life.

Figure 5

```
LIFE
at its
highest
potential
```

Let us return now to our previous illustration. (See figure 5). Notice that the course of the solid line has now become altered. The inner sense of condemnation generated by rejection and self-dislike has been, in itself, enough to serve as a drag or burden, which has altered the course of life. His direction has changed. He has veered off course, away from life at its highest potential. This represents a departure from the original course and from the original destination. It is a departure from life and its abundance; fullness of joy, highest of realization, and satisfaction. Not only is it a departure, but there is an estrangement from the best-possible self, from the ideal which was intended by the Creator.

Condemnation Necessary?

It is interesting that the ancient Hebrews occasionally used the same word to denote a "curse" or a "blessing." The word barok could mean either. Only the context in which the word was used could determine the meaning. In Job 2:9, it is recorded that Job' s wife encouraged him to, "Curse God and die." Another possible interpretation of that passage could have been, "Bless God and die." Only the context determined which meaning the word had. This seems to point to an awareness by even the ancient people of long ago that the interpretation of a given experience determines whether it is made a destructive or a constructive, beneficial one – whether the experience is a curse or a blessing. The meaning it has to us depends on how we respond.

One of my former counselees was sexually molested by her father on several occasions when she was a child. From this and several other experiences and circumstances in which she was reared, some schools of deterministic psychology would have predicted that she would have lived a life filled with hatred for men and probably would have turned to prostitution. Instead, she became a devoted wife and mother deeply involved in community efforts to help girls in trouble. Refusing to be eternally cursed by her early experiences, she used them to become a more compassionate human being. Her cursed experiences taught her about pain, fear, anger, and humiliation. With the help of God, she blessed the lives of hundreds of others.

A person is not automatically cursed by potentially damning events of early life. The person will usually be influenced by them, but how one uses them will determine whether the results are harmful or beneficial. But a child is young, and has little experience in adjusting to painful happenings. Therefore, these damning experiences have a negative influence until they are dealt with and beneficial applications are discovered and used. Change is always a possibility.

The popular belief that childhood is one long chain of happy carefree days linked by peaceful, undisturbed nights appears to be a concept fostered by idealistic dreamers who have lost contact with a painful dimension of reality. Childhood is more typically a period of frustration and turmoil. It is a period that calls for the making of decisions -- decisions that must be made when the person is least equipped by knowledge and experience to perceive the potential outcome of the choices made.

He is deciding: How honest will I be? Will I lie? Under what conditions? Will I steal? Will I accept love? Will I give it? Will I obey the voices of authority? How much will I intentionally hurt others? Will I carry grudges? Will I retaliate? Will I forgive? Is it safe to vent anger? How much? To whom? The questions continue, and the answers continue. There is probably no time in life when we were less prepared for the task of making such decisions. But the act of living required us to make them.

Chapter 4

We Become Criminals

The fact that we are maturing -- that we are becoming persons require the exercise of our decision-making capacity. But the wise decision as well as the foolish decision often makes us into a criminal even in our own eyes.

On the Horns of a Dilemma

Not only must we choose which values to write into our system, but the very fact that we exist sometimes requires us to choose to follow one value to the neglect of another. This places us in a predicament. No choice will be wholly right in our own judgment. Philosophers like to talk about "man's existential predicament." This is a part of it. Life requires that we make decisions, and many decisions – many choices place us in an awful predicament. When we make a decision, we cut off the potential alternatives. When we say "yes" to one, we say "no" to the other options. At this particular moment, I ought to be preparing a lecture, and I ought to be visiting the family of a boy who has been shot in the head with a .38 caliber pistol. I ought also to be playing catch with a fatherless boy, and I ought to be helping my wife put up Christmas decorations. But I have chosen to spend this moment writing at the computer, cutting off all of those and other possible good uses of this particular moment. As a deciding, self-determining organism, I live constantly amid my own value conflicts.

Thomas Oden said it well. "Every pursued good implies a dozen unpursued goods. Every moment spent on the achievement of one goal is time lost on the achievement of numerous other potential goals. I cannot be a chooser without being a denier. . . . Every choice in a sense is a tragic choice, since it is impossible to be a human being without choosing and it is impossible to choose without the negation of value and it is impossible to negate values without guilt. (Oden, pp.44 & 46.)

Despite my best efforts I become guilty! While we are busy evaluating our own behavior, others, important to us are evaluating it also. They, too, are also passing their judgment. While the negative is difficult for the adult, it seems even more painful for the child.

Many children rarely hear approval of those choices that the authorities think are "good," but they will hear of those they think are "bad!" No matter how hard the child may try, the typical child probably will never feel that he can gain total approval. He does fail! He does forget! He is clumsy! He is not perfect! He is negatively judged for that lack, and judgment comes down upon him as condemnation. Bearing a load of condemnation, he is indeed "bent toward sinning." He is falling short of the mark set for him by the authority figures, and he is stirred to angry rebellion by their expectations and his own frustrations.

A Call to Insurrection

While one part of the personality is forming the internal behavioral code, another part begins a reaction. "I don't like it. I don't want it. I won't live by it." An internal insurrection -- a revolt against government, is in the making. Some want to insist that it is only a rebellious facet of one's own personality, while others insist on the influence of some outside personality. They insist on the reality of a personalized opponent to God and man, enticing man toward destruction. Such a being has been given numerous names. Some call him Lucifer. Others call him the Adversary, or the Accuser, or the Father of Lies, or the Opponent, or the Enemy, or the Separator, or the Tempter. Still others call him the Devil while others call him Satan. There is little question that the modern mind has generally rejected the existence of a Satanic, spiritual evil personality. Early in the twenty-first century only 59% of North Americans believe in the existence of a personal Devil.

It seems ironic that at a period in which religious belief so generally rejects belief in the reality of a Satanic personality, organized worship of Satan appears to be at an all-time high. By the late 1960s, Anton Levey, a widely recognized Satanist leader claimed that Satanism had expanded into an international movement of the first magnitude. (LeVey, p.13) Early in the twenty-first century, it continues to grow as "the church of Satan." The internet abounds with more information about it than most of my readers are likely to want to know.

Is it possible that there truly exists an evil, seductive personality who seeks to deceive, to accuse, and to entice toward personal destruction? The Biblical book of Genesis speaks of such a personality. He is described as "subtle," a tanner's word meaning "to debark," as in the debarking or stripping of a tree of its protective and life-sustaining cover. Jesus spoke of him and even encountered him as "the Tempter." Is it possible that he still comes as the tempter, dissuading from the moral, helpful, constructive, beneficial way of life? Is he still subtly stripping human beings of their dignity and sense of worth?

From somewhere comes an "accuser" who taunts, "You are already evil and no-good. You may as well do worse than you have done, or at least repeat what you have already done wrong." Is such a condemnation purely the inner voice of the self? Or is it the voice of a devil? Some would insist it comes from a god. Even the small child may feel a sense of condemnation for his forbidden impulses, and the voice of persuasion within him says, "You're no good. You thought it. You may as well do it. It's not going to hurt you. It's not really important that you live up to the law if you are convinced you can get away with it."

Obscured Omnipotence

We may be seeing the fruit of the seeds of omnipotence of the self, planted shortly after birth and cultivated throughout infancy and early childhood. The newborn has only to open his mouth and yell to get what he wants. The giants in his world may be far bigger than he, but he controls them by simply making his wishes known. If hungry, he yells. The giants feed him. If thirsty, he does the same thing. If they feed him when he wants water, he simply spits it out and screams. The giants frantically search for something different. If they are still wrong, he just yells again and they "hop to" and try to find what he wants. Only when he is satisfied do they get any peace. He seems to be able to make his whole world turn. They may be bigger, but it is he who is in control.

His mere wish can make things happen. He grows accustomed to getting what he wants when he wants it. It is quite common for this feeling of superiority to be carried on into adulthood. It is usually kept as a frightening secret, and masked by the outward evidence of an "inferiority complex." He may even continue through life with the fear that it was his secret wish that caused a parent to die; his secret anger really caused a brother's sickness or accident; or his secret anger might even destroy the whole world. If, by coincidence, the pre-adolescent has a frightening wish to become true, the reinforced feeling of omnipotence may be carried throughout his life.

Harold's father often abused his entire family. As an eight-year-old boy, Harold stood in the window watching his father leave for work and wished that "the old devil would never come back." His father was killed accidentally later that day. And Harold felt somehow responsible. Thirty years later, a man was racing a car down the street in a residential neighborhood. Harold thought, "I wish that S.O.B would wreck." A moment later the car swerved and hit a utility pole. Harold confided, "I am afraid to wish for anything. I'm afraid my wishing will make it come true." My experience, and the experience of others with whom I have shared this interest, has caused me to highly suspect that the secret fear of omnipotence, generated in childhood, is commonly carried into adulthood. But the feeling of omnipotence in children seems to be near-universal.

There seems to be at least a remote correlation between this feeling and the Genesis story of Adam and Eve's temptation. "Follow your own inclinations and 'you will be like God, omnipotent and omniscient, knowing good and evil'" (cf. Gen. 3:5). To this point in our discussion of preadolescence, only "good" is known by personal, intimate acquaintance. "Knowledge" was used in the Bible in reference to the intimacy of sexual intercourse and even today we use the term "carnal knowledge." We begin life knowing only "good." But we did not stay that way for long. By the willful violation of the sense of "ought", we become intimately acquainted with evil too.

One More Fall

The child's feelings of inadequacy and all the added feelings of condemnation are painful. Like other members of the animal family, he typically responds to pain with fear or anger. Both fear and anger have a way of blinding to reality. Compensating, he assumes a false sense of adequacy that includes an arrogant type of pride, "Regardless of what anyone says, I'll do what I want, when I want." He tends to rebel against every authority -- even authority he has earlier vested in himself as lawmaker.

He seems to regret having agreed with the voices of authority who said "you ought." The ink is barely dry on the pages of the internal code-book before his role as legislator is changed to that of criminal. He violates his own adopted code of behavior: "I know I told myself I would not lie, but a lie may get me out of trouble." Or, "I told myself I would not steal, but I wanted the toy." Deep within himself, he knows he has chosen less than the best. He knows that he is responsible for his deception and his feelings of guilt arise from the knowledge that he could have and should have acted otherwise. He will choose less than the most constructive, again and again throughout his life. And each time he does, he loses something of worth.

In a television presentation of A Man for All Seasons, Sir Thomas Moore was presented as having said that there is a very real sense in which a man holds himself very delicately in his own hands. He has to but open his own fingers in the betrayal of his own values and he thereby loses himself.

Why Is Right, Right and Wrong, Wrong?

We live in a day in which everything is considered relative. You probably have been told or you may even have told others that no universal rights and wrongs exist. It is commonly believed, "All right and wrong is relative to the culture in which you live. That which is right in one culture is wrong in another." Only those with the most superficial, surface understanding of various cultures can believe that no universal values exist within the human race.

We might be able to think more clearly, with less passion, if we look at "right" and "wrong" on the basis of the consequences *rather than on the basis of opinion.* It appears that every moral/ethical value that God has given is based on one major principle: if a behavior harms any person -- degrades, or takes from one's life, the behavior is classified as "wrong" or "bad" -- immoral, thereby making one truly guilty. A good that one recognizes that needs to be done, but is neglected makes one truly guilty. The New Testament book of James says it clearly. "To the person who knows to do good and does not do it, to that person, it is sin. (cf. Jas. 4:17).

Behavior and attitude that uplifts, strengthens, encourages, or works toward life or a higher quality of life is called "right" or "good," thereby leaving one without guilt. Borrowing on this Biblical principle, a renowned psychiatrist of another era called this the basic philosophy of "Bioethics."

Good is all that serves life; evil is all that serves death. Good is reverence for life, all that enhances life, growth unfolding. Evil is all that stifles life, narrows it down, cut into pieces. . . . The conscience of the biophilous person is not one of forcing oneself to refrain from evil and to do good, It is not the superego described by Freud, which is a strict taskmaster, employing sadism against oneself for the sake of virtue. The biophilous conscience is motivated by its attraction to life and to joy; the moral effort consists in strengthening the life-loving side in oneself. For this reason the biophil does not dwell in remorse and guilt which, after all, are only aspects of self-lothing and sadness. He turns quickly to life and attempts to do good. (Fromm, p.47)

A serious study of the ethical teachings that grow out of all the world's great religions suggest that at their foundation is the basic principle of this philosophy that says, "good" serves life and "evil" serves death to the personality. Each of these cultures seem to use this principle as it builds its code of ethics upon its understanding of what contributes to life and its understanding of what contributes to death. We appear to be looking at the foundation of universal values that transcend culture and is etched into the very heart of humankind.

In doing so, we should be able to point to some universal "rights and wrongs." If that which contributes to life is basically "good" and that which contributes to death is basically "evil," then the most basic evil would be the killing of a human being -- not necessarily the physical death, but the murder of the personality -- any personality -- one's own or that of another.

Even if we were considering only the taking of the physical life, the principle would still apply. Someone will quickly object, "But there are groups, even whole cultures that not only kill freely, but take pride in doing so." But can you imagine a culture that tolerates killing just anyone, even one's own tribesman just because he or she has the urge to kill?

But we are looking at more than the taking of the physical life. We are looking at that which destroys the very soul -- the personality – the character -- the "humanness" of the human being. We are talking of that which contributes to the decay, the coarsening of the spirit, the rot of the heart with greed, envy, hatred, and unfaithfulness.

We are looking at that which is "pro-death" over against that which is "pro-life." It is upon this pro-life pro-death principle that all values art built. Laws of "fairness," laws of "loyalty," and laws of "rights" all have behind them a universal value -- a value held by humankind. Consider the words of the respected philosopher, former atheist-turned-Christian, C.S. Lewis:

I know that some people say the idea of a Law of Nature or decent behavior known to all men is unsound, because different civilizations and different ages have had quite different moralities. But this is not true. There have been differences between moralities, but these have never amounted to anything like total differences. If anyone will take the trouble to compare the moral teachings of say, the ancient Egyptians, Babylonians, Hindus, Chinese, Greeks and Romans, what will really strike him will be how very like they are to each other and to our own. . .

Think what a totally different morality would mean. Think of a country where people were admired for running away in battle, or where a man felt proud of double crossing all the people who had been kindest to him. Men have differed as regards to what people you ought to be unselfish to . . . but . . . selfishness has never been admired. (Lewis, p.19)

If there is such a thing as a universal value, it would, indeed seem to be based on the "pro-life" principle: That which pulls man away from death, building upward, inclining toward life, we call "good." And that which deteriorates from life, pulling toward death being that which is considered "bad."

From where does such a basic value, written into the very fabric of humankind, originate? That question makes little more sense than the question that asks, "From where does the capacity for reason originate?" Though we cannot answer these questions with certainty that satisfies all minds, we do know that both, human capacity for reasoning, and the capacity for moral judgments are possible because of the part of the brain called the neocortex. Many insist that it is this unique human possession that differentiates us from all other animals. This unique portion of the brain seems to make humans what we are – human. It is there, in the neocortex that we make moral decisions. There we evaluate attitudes and actions before and after the fact. There we experience satisfaction with ourselves, or there we feel guilt. There resides our inclinations toward life or toward death – toward good or toward evil – toward that which is constructive of personality or toward that which is erosive of personality.

Parents who truly love their children teach behavior by their words and their values by their actions. The loving parent, by the highest form of love, teaches their children to behave in pathways that are constructive and away from pathways that are destructive to the body or to the personality. But children disobey.

Disobedience Equates Lack of Faith

Most people in the child's tiny world have greater knowledge and experience than the child. But out of a sense of self-centered pride the children often disregard efforts that have been made to communicate the best way for contented, constructive life. When instruction is given to keep children and even adults from harming themselves, they tend to say, "I know best. No one is going to tell me what to do. I'll do what I want to do when I want to do it. I am wise enough to know what is best for me. My source of instruction is not to be trusted. I'll trust only my own inclinations. I will accept none as wiser or greater than I." Indeed, we are looking at a form of idolatry by which people try to make themselves the god of their own world; the ultimate authority in their lives.

When the child rejects parental authority saying, "I'll touch the poison ivy if I want to," or "I'll eat the whole bottle of aspirin if I want to," he is stepping out on his own in violation of another law: a law against bringing harm to any human being -- one's self' or another. He violates the law of love. But his crime is not against a law. His true crime is against persons -- others and himself. Theft demeans the thief while it takes from the owner. The lie may harm another, but it debases the liar. His willful disobedience to his own pre-established law and/or to constructive outside authority has contributed to his moving away from the route of life to its highest possible good.

When approaching the idea of good or bad (constructive or destructive) behavior, relating it to some outside authority, some minds turn immediately to their concept of a god. One may choose to declare that since he does not believe in the existence of a God, a Cosmic Father, he can do exactly as he chooses without being harmed. But the results are still the same. Some actions always bring harm to oneself and/or to others. Poison is still poison, no matter who calls attention to it. It is still poison, even if no one calls attention to the truth. And the degree of intent does not change the toxic results. Poison deflects away from life.

It seems best to pause to consider figure 6.

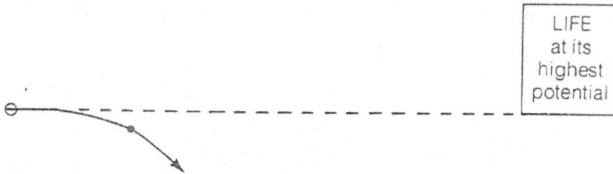

Figure 6

LIFE
at its
highest
potential

From the course toward life at its highest potential, the first deflection occurred in "conditioned badness," resulting in condemnation even though the child was yet innocent. The second deflection is the results of willful rebellion against authority, including disobedience to one's own adopted code of behavior. *That which is away from life is toward death.*

Movement Toward Death

Though generally not recognized, a quiet destructive process has been set into action. The violator is no longer the person he was before the violation. He is less than he was. His highest potential for personhood has been damaged. A tiny part of His humanity has eroded away. He may now be somewhat compared to a pie with a tiny piece torn away. A part of him is destroyed.

(See Figure 7.) Each time he does that which harms any person or fails to do good when he knew he had the opportunity to do so, a tiny bit more of the person is eroded away.

Figure 7

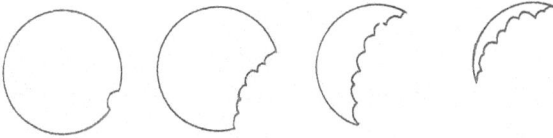

Departure from the way to life's highest potential may be referred to as being "lost." One is lost from the way of the most constructive and healthful route of life. Rejecting outside authority, he is on his own, without a guiding star or a compass. He has neither the wisdom of those who have walked before him, nor experience of his own by which he may set a course.

Even when he should learn by his own experience, he will often return to repeat the former error. Every day, we see those persons who fail to learn from their mistakes. Men dying of lung cancer, will light their cigarette and blow smoke with all but their last breath, insisting, "Nobody is going to tell me how to live my life." Truly, broad is the way that leads to destruction. In the process, a man with this attitude will die with a sense of pride: "At least I did it my way." He may have harmed himself and degraded himself and he may have brought suffering to those who crossed his path, but he generates a sense of virtue in having done it his way. "I accept no authority beyond myself," he says boastfully. Many wonder what he has to be proud of. It is no accident of language that someone may say of him that "he is a person who lacks "integrity." The dictionary says the word means adherence to a code of moral value, or the quality of being completed." By failing to adhere to even his own code of moral value, he is becoming less complete: thus, he lacks "integrity," or you may say that he is becoming "disintegrated"; that is, he is falling apart, moving toward death.

The ancient Greeks recognized that humans enjoy two forms of life. When they wrote or spoke of our physical life, they referred to our bios. When they wrote or spoke of our spiritual life, they used the word zoe. On the day we first took of the forbidden fruit, we can be assured, we began to die. The "big lie" told to every person in every age denies this truth. "You will not surely die" (Gen. 3:4), " . . . Indulge in the seven deadly sins as they need hurt no one" (LeVey, p.85). "You cannot really be harmed by the things you do in violation of moral law," says the teacher of modern satanic worship. However, the Bible teaches it and study of human behavior insists that the violation of God's law or the violation of our own adopted moral code always works to destroy the zoe – the spiritual life, and violations often work to destroy the bios – the physical life.

Let's pause and examine one of the Ten Commandments – the one that says we must not steal. Let's suppose that you and I are traveling together. We stop to spend a night in a motel. While you are bathing, I spot your wallet or purse. I open it and see that you have several hundreds of dollars. I take out ten dollars, confident that you will not miss it. If you do, you will assume that you have simply lost track of how much you have spent. You certainly will not suspect that I have taken it. Who will have been harmed?

Of course, you will have lost a small part of that for which you have earned from your labor, which represents a small part of your time – a small part of your life. You will have been harmed. But what of me? I will have robbed myself of something worth far more than the ten dollars I have taken from you. I will have eroded a precious part of me. If I had resisted the temptation to steal, I would have grown stronger. But when I failed to resist the temptation and stole from you, I am now weaker. Since I am weaker, it will be easier for me to steal again. When I steal again, I will be even weaker, with less ability to resist the temptation to steal. Each time I steal, more of me is eroded and I become more and more vulnerable to the temptation to steal. Wanting only the best for His people, more than three thousand years ago, God saw His people harming themselves and others. Being the loving Father that He is, He wanted his people not to harm themselves. He gave them Ten Commandments in His efforts to lead them away from damaging behaviors and to constructive behaviors. Each violation of each law brings its own natural consequence.

If I lie, I damage me as much or more than I damage others. If I commit adultery, I damage me and the person with whom I commit adultery. If I place any god above Jehovah, the Father of Jesus Christ, I will follow a god of lesser values which will result in behavior that harms me and/or others. God does not have to punish us. Life punishes us by eroding a precious part of ourselves. (Look again to figure 7.) What is eroded? What is harmed? What is damaged? What begins dying? What is in danger of being destroyed? One's humanity! One's personality! One's character! One's self! One's soul – that which makes him who he is -- that which God intended to live forever with Him!

That which distinguished him from the other animals begins to die. The more disintegrated, the more degenerated he becomes, the more animal-like he becomes. We err when we try to equate "humanity" with the "animal," and we err when we to speak of one who acts immorally, that is, one who harms or degrades another or himself, as being "merely human." The phrase is almost always associated with the base, degenerate, animal-like behavior. It is away from his human qualities that he turns to become more animal. Indeed, the character of some of the higher animals would be insulted if accused of some man's degenerative acts and attitudes. One's humanity is dying. His spiritual dimension is dying.

The "Law of Mortigression"

In addition to this deterioration, unknown to him, he has quietly become the victim of the "law of Mortigression," a law as old as humankind and as reliable as the law of gravity or the law of momentum. Laws of nature were written into the foundation of the universe at the beginning. Laws related to gravity, to friction, to heat transfer, to the behavior of liquids, and other laws are studied in every basic course in physics.

To understand the Law of Mortigression, it may help to look at some phenomena of nature. First, consider an eroding hillside. With each rain, soil is washed away. With each freeze, the surface expands, loosens, and is made more vulnerable to the rains and winds that follow. The process is typically slow and generally unnoticeable until the larger scars one day are obvious. Those who have flown over Southern Oklahoma have seen this kind of erosion in its extreme form. The Grand Canyon is an even more obvious illustration. The next natural phenomenon to consider is the bolder rolling down a hill. The faster it rolls, the faster it rolls, and the more difficult it is to stop. Momentum wants to keep it going. The Law of Momentum is roughly stated, "A body at rest tends to remain at rest, and a body in motion tends to remain in motion unless acted upon by an outside source." Now, let's pull these facts of nature together. That which erodes, detracts, or takes away from life may be compared to the rain or wind eroding, taking away from our hillside, making it less and less than it was before. It is disintegrating. It washes away with nothing to stop the process, somewhat like the boulder rolling down the hill. In reality, the tiny particles of soil are but miniature boulders. A man who lives in the edge of the Great Smoky Mountain National Park told of having been in the mountains fishing for trout when a sudden summer "cloudburst" dumped its rain on the mountains above. Having lived in those mountains most of his life, when he heard a thunderous noise, he fled the stream to higher ground, barely escaping the avalanche of water and boulders, some as big as automobiles, rolling, bouncing down the mountainside as if they were mere pebbles.

Calling upon the law of momentum, we are reminded that the particles of soil, or boulders that will continue down the hillside unless acted upon by an outside force. But it is not the ongoing movement of the soil or the boulders that we are primarily concerned with at this moment. Our concern is with the erosive process. The actual erosive process itself will continue on and on unless acted upon by some outside force.

Geologists tell us that millions of years ago, the Smoky Mountains of the Appalachian chain were hundreds, if not thousands of feet taller than they are today. Erosion has been eating them away, somewhat analogous to the pie of figure 7. Having lived in the region of those mountains for more than forty years, I have witnessed their erosion by thousands of tons of soil and rocks. Land-slides and rock-slides occur almost every year, sometimes closing Interstate Highway 40.

Drawing on all of these parallels of nature, we might recognize that similar to the law of momentum, *A personality in the process of disintegration tends to continue in the process of disintegration unless acted upon by an outside force.* This, I call the "Law of Mortigression." The student of Latin will immediately recognize the literal translation of this word "mortigression" as the law of "movement toward death." This process happens even when no *feelings* of guilt are present in any form!

During the days I was writing this chapter a dejected young woman wept as she looked across my desk.
She said, "Two years ago I destroyed myself."
I asked, "What do you mean?"

"I don't know how to say it any other way. When I started abusing the use of drugs and sex and alcohol and stole, taking all of that as my way of life, I destroyed me."

Such destruction of human life is criminal! One person destroys the life qualities within himself by his greed. Another damages himself by abuse of alcoholic drink. Another does it with a grudge he carries day by day as it eats away at his soul and damages his heart. Another destroys his life by excessive toil, and his neighbor accomplishes the same kind of destruction by his excessive play. St. Augustine referred to such behavior as "murder (of) the real human being." (tr. Pusey, p.27) Murder is a criminal act whether against another or oneself. And we judge ourselves for each contribution made toward accomplishing any murder.

Chapter 5

We Go On Trial

For each violation of our own adopted code of behavior, we conduct an inner trial. Some trials may go on and on. Others last only a moment. To help make some important matters clear, I'll share with you two of my own experiences in that inner courtroom.

On Trial in My Own Courtroom

I had weighed the issues, passed the bills into law, and concluded that I had violated my own established code of behavior. Not only had my attention been arrested, alerted, and focused on my failure, but I too had been arrested – arrested in the sense of "having been stopped," failing to fulfill – falling short of what I could have become. I was to make myself stand trial for my failure. I should have expected little justice and less mercy. I knew immediately that I didn't have a chance to be vindicated. It was rigged – little more than a kangaroo court.

My eyes swept the courtroom. The judge was already on the bench. He must have had a bad day. He looked mean and angry. There sat the Court Recorder. He had nothing to say, but you could bet he wasn't going to miss a word. Everything would go into the record. At least he looked kind enough. If the case against me sounded too bad, perhaps he would bury it in the memory bank to make it hard to find later. That was a comforting thought.

I'd just as soon have forgotten the whole ordeal anyway. The arresting officer sat reading his little black book. He was sure to have every detail of my violation. He wouldn't leave out a thing. The prosecuting attorney looked disgustingly confident, and it was obvious that he was impatient. He had a good case, and he was eager to see me convicted.

A fresh wave of anxiety swept over me. I felt sick. As I was ushered to my seat, I could feel my knees getting weak. I was glad to sit down by the side of my defense counsel. He didn't look very happy either. He would try hard. I could at least depend on that. He knew I was in for a hard time, but he had a lot of legal maneuvers up his sleeve. I didn't care what he did or said. I didn't want to be convicted.

The courtroom was packed. Everybody wanted in on the proceeding. I began to panic. They weren't just idle curiosity seekers! They were witnesses for the prosecution! The whole cloud of witnesses was against me.

I finally mustered the courage to look at the panel of jurors. They were a grim-looking bunch. Not a friendly face in the crowd. I got the feeling they weren't even interested in hearing all the evidence. They would have preferred to vote me "guilty" immediately to get it over with. As I surveyed the courtroom again, I had the shocking realization that every person in the room had the same face. My face! They were all a faction of me.

Every person has his own inner courtroom, and every face there is his own, a further indication of his fragmentation (cf. Mark 5:9). It is to the inner courtroom that we take ourselves for every violation of every law we have set up for ourselves to obey. If we are even reasonably mentally healthy, there are no exceptions. I go there often. I have long done so and I will continue to go there for as long as I live. And so will every person.

The pounding of the judge's gavel pulled me back from my reflections. The judge called the court to order and began reading the charge against me. "The defendant is charged with the violation of his own Internal Value Code. On or about September 5, he and his father were building a house. While following his father across the yard, he did have the fleeting impulse to strike his father in the head with a hammer."

I could feel my face redden. Tears burned my eyes and my heart pounded in my ears as I glanced uneasily about the room. Every head was wagging with dismay. I overheard one of the witnesses saying, "And he seemed to be such a nice boy. Can you imagine him having such evil thoughts against such a fine man as his father?" "And that man loves him, too."

Somebody else leaned over and whispered, "I know it happened. I was there." Condemned, and the trial was just beginning. The buzz of gossip ended only when the judge pounded the gavel and called for order.

Looking down on me, the judge growled, "Boy, what's your plea? Guilty or not guilty?" Before I could open my mouth, my defense counsel spoke out, "Not guilty Your Honor. In fact, we respectfully move that the case be immediately dismissed on the grounds that my client did not really have the impulse to hit his father in the head; there just happened to be a mosquito on his father's bald spot." "Dismissal denied." The judge added sarcastically, "Come now, counselor, you're going to have to do better than that."

The defense mechanism called "denial" is one of the most common means of escape from the screams of an accusing conscience and the frightening sense of impending punishment. It often works well for at least a short while. The mental gymnastics required to persuade oneself that he really did, or thought, or felt no wrong are truly remarkable. It seems doubtful that any creature other than man has so thoroughly mastered the capacity for self-deception.

"If we say that we have not sinned, we make him (God) a liar, and his word is not in us" (I John 1:10). (As a side interest here, if one is at all successful in self-deception, at a lower level of consciousness he recognizes that he has lied. Having perjured himself, he must be tried in the inner courtroom for the additional offense.)

We will try one mechanism of defense after another in an effort to quiet the accusing conscience. We search for the one that is most likely to help. Something must be done to deaden the accusing cries, to relieve that dread of punishment, and to keep from hearing a verdict of "guilty." This anxiety can be one of the most severe pains. We become aware of this pain early in life, and many find it useful. Note that I did not say "constructive" – I said *useful*. Anxiety may well have its constructive elements at times, but it also has a destructive use. We will return to this destructive use of anxiety later, but now we need to get back to the trial.

The judge, shaking his head impatiently, looked rather disgusted as he turned his attention from my defense counselor. "Mr. Prosecutor, are you ready to present your case?"

As the first witness to the stand, my defense counselor took me by the arm and led me quickly from the courtroom. He was not only helping to delay my trial, he was an expert at directing my mind from the conflict. He headed for the baseball park while the radio blared the latest music. I whistled loudly and sang every song I could remember; I worked hard to recall every word. During the game, I concentrated on every move of every player and even memorized their names and numbers. Between innings, I computed the batting averages, and during every pause I labored to memorize them. As we drove from the parking lot, I settled into my seat and entered into one of my favorite fantasies, imagining I was a fighter pilot in the cockpit of my aircraft on a mission over enemy territory. The sky was filled with enemy fighters intent on destroying the bomber squadron I was there to defend. Of course, they were no challenge to a skilled ace such as I. One enemy aircraft after another was blasted out of the sky, and the last of the enemy was seen trailing smoke as it disappeared on the horizon. I was sleepy by this time and dozed the rest of the way home.

Exhausted, I stumbled to bed, pulled up the covers, and drifted into the world of dreams, only to awaken in terror as I fled the attack of a large black bear. My attention was immediately arrested, and I was quickly ushered back into my inner courtroom. The judge glanced my way shaking his head as if to say, "You didn't, really expect to get away with all of those diversions, did you?" My defense counselor leaned over and smiled, "Oh, well, it worked for a while. If we are careful, we might be able to get out of here with a few more diversionary trips before this trial is over."

Let's pause again as we consider these activities. The defense mechanism of distraction succeeds temporarily as the attention is diverted from the voice of condemnation and the pointing finger of the inner accuser. Diversion of the mind into the world of fantasy, escape into excessive sleep, and distraction by recreation are among the devices used to escape the pain of the accusing conscience. Of course, the purpose of this mechanism of defense is to busy the mind with anything other than the violation and the accusations made by the conscience. I'm not suggesting that all such activity is an attempt to escape the cries of an uneasy conscience, but they are commonly used for this purpose.

Let's return to the trial. I was now fully awake, and the prosecuting attorney was continuing the accusations: "Gentlemen of the jury, you will notice that the defendant thought he could avoid your judgment of 'guilty' by simply refusing to listen to the witnesses against him. You must surely be concluding already that he is, indeed, guilty and that He did have the fleeting impulse to strike his father."

Each witness took the stand to tell essentially the same story, with little to add and nothing to weaken the case against me. At last, the prosecution rested its case.

My defense counsel approached the jury. "Gentlemen, surely you would not convict such a fine young boy. Look at his conduct since the time of the alleged offense. He has helped his father willingly. He has shown far more love for his father than most boys his age. He is obedient in almost everything and is showing himself to be a boy his father can be proud to call his son. . . ." The judge impatiently interrupted. "Counselor, what has this to do with the charge against your client? You are talking about his behavior since the time of the violation. That has nothing to do with his crime."

In desperation, my defense counsel pleaded, "But Your Honor, Gentlemen of the jury, surely you aren't going to convict my client! That's just the way he is. Surely he is not to be punished for having been born with such an urge? We could bring in any number of psychiatrists who would witness that almost every boy occasionally experiences hostile impulses toward his father."

The judge simply shook his head and turned to the jury: "It is obvious that counsel for the defense has no defense to present. The fact that the boy has compensated for his impulse by being extremely obedient, abundantly loving, and more than a willing helper, has nothing to do with guilt or innocence. Such common mechanisms of defense are practiced in every inner court in an effort to gain an acquittal. The claim that he was born with such an urge is one of the most common defenses men use to avoid admitting responsibility. I must remind you that nothing alters the fact that he did have the impulse to strike his father in the head with a hammer!"

Before the judge could continue, the foreman of the jury stood up. "Your Honor, I beg you to pardon the intrusion, but this jury has heard about as much of this case as we can stand. We have no need to deliberate. He is guilty as charged." Suddenly the courtroom seemed wild. Everyone was screaming, "Guilty, Guilty, Guilty!" The judge, the jury, the prosecutor, the recorder, and the courtroom full of witnesses were all pointing their finger at me and shouting their condemnation. Added to the cries of "guilty" was the demand, "Pay! Make him pay! Give him what he deserves!" The judge demanded order. A hush fell over the courtroom as he leaned forward, scowling down upon me. He directed me to rise to hear my punishment.

''You will pay! You will pay a fine by relinquishing a portion of your dignity, your self-respect, and your sense of worth. You will feel ill-at-ease and worthless." My knees gave way beneath me. I sank heavily into my chair. What was I to do? There was no choice. I had to pay. The loss from my sense of worth was terrible. But that kind of hurt was becoming familiar. I was experiencing it again and again, following every pronouncement of "guilty" that my inner judge declared. Of course, nothing is unusual about that. It is one of the most common of man's experiences.

I felt heavy and tired, but I had to get out of there. I didn't know it at the time, but every conviction of guilt becomes a weighty burden, draining both emotional and physical energy. A truism has been passed around from time to time, "Every person has his bag." Guilt is a part of the load that we carry in our "bag," and it commonly results in perpetual fatigue. Doctors hear it as one of the most common complaints. Victims of guilt drag from physician to physician, trying to get relief. "Doctor, I'm tired all the time. I sleep all night but I wake up as tired as I was when I went to bed." Numerous tests fail to confirm any physical illness.

The doctor may suggest that the tired body is a physical response to an emotional stress, but too often he is reluctant to make a referral to a qualified therapist. He is afraid his patient will respond as if he were being called "crazy." Even the doctor with the courage to express this suspicion of emotional stress may refer to the psychotherapist as a "nerve doctor." Many people find it easier to speak of themselves as having a problem with their "nerves" than to admit inner conflicts. Among the most common of inner conflicts are those involving guilt.

And my own inner warfare was growing more and more painful all the time. As I came out of the courtroom I happened to glance toward a mirror hanging by the door. To my dismay, I saw how dirty I was. I was stained – impure -- defiled. Since I knew of no way to cleanse myself, I could only hang my head in shame and go on my way.

Guilt commonly leaves us feeling as though we were literally dirty, in need of a bath. A classic example is found in Shakespear's tragedy, Macbeth (Act 5, sc.1). An accomplice in murder, Lady Macbeth nightly paced the castle grounds, wringing her hands and crying, "Out, damned spot," as she struggled to wash from her hands the traces of blood that only she could see and feel. In my own experience in counseling with those tormented by guilt, I have heard some say they regularly bathe from four to six times daily, trying to scrub away the "dirty feeling." The "damned spot" covers the whole person. Soap and water give only a few moments of relief. Even given the best of more than 380 cleaning agents available on the supermarket shelves, what could wash away such guilt as that for which I had just been tried and convicted?

I stepped outside and observed that the sun seemed not as bright as before. A feeling of depression gripped me. But why? Why do we feel "down" after our inner judge declares us to be guilty? There are at least two reasons. First, we experience grief, an emotion accompanying the loss of someone or some thing cherished. Here, I had just experienced loss to my dignity and sense of worth. I was experiencing sorrow in the face of such a loss. Also, I was sad as I faced my damaged self-image. My behavior had been inconsistent with my picture of who I am. I feel pain when I see the split between who I am and who I ought to be.

And we experience anger. We get angry with ourselves – angry for being so weak – angry for having violated our adopted code. Any anger not adequately expressed usually converts into depression. Out of such anger comes a sense of alienation, a feeling of being cut off from one who is angry with us. And when the one angry with us happens to be our self, we can, and usually do, feel alienated from ourselves. We may be quite accepting, even forgiving, of similar behavior by someone else, but we tend to expect more of ourselves. Most of us are less forgiving of ourselves than we are of others. "I ought to be above such thoughts, feelings, or actions," we insist.

It should be emphasized that the preceding courtroom drama followed a mere impulse, a fleeting thought with an accompanying feeling – so fleeting that it would barely classify in most minds as a temptation. Those who study the psychological development of children would generally agree that such an impulse as described in the foregoing trial is typical. Yet the child usually will condemn himself for such an impulse even when there is absolutely no overt act toward fulfilling the impulse.

It is possible for us to feel as guilty for having thought something as we may feel for having done something that violates our moral code. The sense of condemnation or "not O.K.ness" for secret thoughts of misbehavior often becomes the motivation for actual misbehavior, as further discussion soon will show.

During the development of the internal code, certain thoughts and feelings were inwardly declared as prohibitive. The preamble to that code of ethics has a clause that reads, ". . . and even to be tempted to violate this code shall carry the equivalency to having accomplished the act." Assault upon a parent and incest are usually on the list of which "Thou shalt not think!" Some religious leaders have magnified this prohibition and have tried to write an eleventh commandment: "Thou shalt fully control thy thoughts and thy feelings and it shall be considered as immoral to have fleeting immoral impulses as it is to perform immoral deeds." They forget that the New Testament speaks of Jesus as having been tempted but did not sin (Heb. 4:15). When the temptation is equated with the deed, the inner court is adjourned for only a few moments. Indeed, the victim usually lives under a perpetual sense of condemnation.

This is one of the major reasons that such a large part of the psychiatric community has been characterized as "anti-religious." They have reacted strongly to the binding of men with an unreal, unreasonable, damaging sense of guilt. The Bible teaches that Christ came to set men free. It is ironic that in His name men have so often tried to bind and control their fellow human beings by the fetters of guilt. Matthew 5:27-29 has commonly been used to pronounce condemnation on persons for even fleeting impulses.

Consider Jesus' words when He said, "Whoever looketh on a woman to lust after her hath committed adultery with her already in his heart." Was He observing a truth, pronouncing a judgment, or was He giving a warning? Or is it possible that He was doing all three at once? Even those who do not accept Jesus' divinity admit that He had a peculiar insight into human thought and feeling. He would have observed that persons tend to feel guilty for the things they think. He saw that we tend to take on some of the burden of guilt for imagined misdeeds. But there is more to his statement than a mere observation.

Jesus came loving, giving a judgment of "good" on that which was constructive to persons and a judgment of "evil" on that which was harmful. He judged adulterous lust as harmful to the individual personality. Since there is an element of control in lust and since the Greek verbs of the verse in question connote *intentional practice,* there is far more involved than the fleeting impulse. A part of the warning is against looking with the intentional purpose of stirring erotic interests. By the time purposeful intent has become a part of the experience, there will have been damage by erosion or degeneration of the personality. If one has lacked only the opportunity to carry out the act of the will, he judges himself as though he had already accomplished it.

But there is at least one complex step between temptation and the intent to fulfill that temptation. It is a step of surrender. We must surrender an amount of personal integrity and we must experience degeneration of moral fiber in order to intend to fulfill a temptation. An adequate definition of the word *lust* requires the element of intent. Desiring only the best for those He loves, Jesus warned against every degree of personal harm. But when men have harmed themselves and others, Jesus has sought to bring healing from the damage by the earliest surrender through the most agonizing consequences of the accomplished deed. Surely, there is nothing to suggest that merely the intent to seduce brings damage equivalent to the complete adulterous seduction. Only one person is involved in the thought or impulse. The woman (for whom the lust is felt) and her family will have gone unaffected in any way, possibly never aware of the secret desire cultivated by the man at some distance. It seems more than obvious that the full extent of the damage to the self and to others is not experienced until the misdeed is enacted.

Keep in mind that the self is aware of every degree of breakdown in personal integrity. The accusing voice of conscience makes its outcry, and there is almost always a conviction. It is unfortunate that many psychologists, psychiatrists, social workers, and trained pastoral counselors have concluded that men are to be made whole by simply silencing the voice of the accuser – the conscience. This "remedy" is as absurd as reducing the fever of pneumonia with aspirin and then pronouncing the patient "cured." As fever is one way the body has of screaming, "Something's physically wrong inside," the miserable, accusing conscience is one way the personality (soul) has of screaming, "Something's spiritually or emotionally wrong inside." (Remember that our words soul, psyche, and psychology come from the same word rooted in the Greek language).

Guilt feeling can be beneficial. It serves as an inner signal, telling us to turn back from a harmful behavior to an uplifting behavior. It serves as a force calling for good. From where does that voice come?

I do not have the wisdom, intuition, or knowledge to say when the accusing voice of conscience is that of the self and when it may be the voice of God. And I am acutely aware that an inner accusing voice may cry out even though there has been no moral violation; that is, that no violation has been committed that would cause harm to anyone, including self. There is, then, room for error, and there is the danger of self-deification by declaring the accusing voice of self to be that of God. Who can say when God speaks or even how He communicates? It seems as presumptuous for me, a theist, to assert that God always speaks by way of conscience as it is for the atheist to assert that there is no God to speak and the voice of conscience is purely a response to earlier teachings.

Before we get too far removed from the earlier courtroom procedure, important matters not yet discussed require that we return to the inner court once again. There are similarities in any criminal court action, but each trial is different. The accusation may be different. The arguments of the defense may be different, but the scene is essentially the same, with the judge, jury, prosecutor, defense counsel, and the observers. (The executioner waits silently.) Each, of course, is a segment of the fragmented self.

The inner court is somewhat comparable to the action of a ventriloquist, projecting not only his own voice but a segment of himself as he responds to the numerous roles of those involved in the drama. Each person speaks inwardly with many voices.

Let's look to another brief trial in my own inner courtroom. The judge read the charge: "William G. Justice, Jr., you are charged with having stolen a U.S. Army Rifle, caliber 30 Carbine from a United States Air Force Squadron Personal Equipment Storeroom. This occurred while you were stationed on Okinawa with the primary responsibility for piloting B-29 bombers. How do you plead? Guilty or not guilty?"

My face flushed and my heart seemed to pound in my ears as the muscles of my stomach tightened. I opened my mouth to respond but could only hang my head in shame. Even my defense counsel sat in silence to the question. The prosecuting attorney plainly stated the details and called for the testimony by the witnesses. They wept as they gave the details. By the way the witnesses carried on, it seemed that I might just as well have swindled a sick widow and her children of their life savings! I could finally lift my head when the prosecutor had rested his case and my defense counselor stood to build my defense.

Defense Counsel: "Your Honor, Gentlemen of the Jury: There were more than twenty-five rifles with no records of serial numbers. No one was accountable for them, and it seemed that all his friends were taking them."

Prosecuting Attorney: "I object; his peers are not on trial here."
Judge: "Objection sustained."
Defense Counsel: "But even some of his superior officers were getting them."
Prosecuting Attorney: "Objection! His superiors are not being tried here either."
Judge: "Objection sustained."

Defense Counsel: "But the military culture in which he lived was responsible. Everyone knows that military personnel often live by a system of 'moonlight requisition,' simply taking government-owned equipment without authorization. Not only that, his peers knew of the availability of those rifles and would have called him 'foolish' or 'chicken' to have failed to take one."

Prosecuting Attorney: "Again I object! The defense counselor is admitting that his client took the rifle. He is only offering excuses for having done so. The defendant can't place the responsibility on others. If we have to listen to this kind of defense, he'll soon be trying to blame his mama and daddy and the fact that he was an economically deprived child of the Depression. He made the choice! He exercised his own will and took the rifle."

Judge: "Objection sustained. Counselor, it is granted that you are stating some of the circumstances surrounding the offense, but it has no bearing on the mounting evidence that he did, without authorization, take the rifle."

Defense Counsel: "But Your Honor, the rifle he took was from the government, one of the world's largest organizations with hundreds of billions of dollars in assets. My client harmed no one. The war in Korea has ended, and these rifles will be practically given away through the war surplus stores. He took it for deer hunting when he returns to civilian life. He has served the United States Air Force well and gets relatively little pay. The government owes him a little extra."

Prosecuting Attorney: "Objection. . . ."

Judge: "Never mind. Mr. Prosecutor, it is obvious that the defense has no valid defense. All the defense has used are the same efforts at rationalization and justification that almost everyone uses." Turning to the jury: "Gentlemen of the jury, I order you to find the defendant 'guilty, as charged.' "

"Guilty! Guilty! Guilty!" The words seemed to echo and settle sickeningly in the pit of my stomach. I wasn't surprised. I knew I was guilty, but I was trying to get out of paying the price. It was just another exercise in futility.

I was convicted once again in my own inner courtroom. This was neither the first nor the last time for me to be under conviction. It was just one among hundreds. Like every convicted criminal, I would remain a convict until my debt was paid.

Note: We must pause and recognize that while there are many with an overly sensitive conscience, there are remnants of personalities who have become so disintegrated that they feel no sense of wrong for even the most outrageous offense. One at this level might dismember a child and experience no more remorse than for killing a fly. Or he might rape and slay a young mother in the presence of screaming children and later joke of his experience. He is a blight to his society, and he presents a problem to any who would try to help him. We will return to this subject within another context.

Chapter 6

We Make Ourselves Pay

Learned Behavior

It is almost universally accepted that violators of a law must "pay" for their offenses by some form of punishment. The world's legal systems are built on this premise. As we earlier examined life under law, we were reminded that "payment by punishment" begins with the harsh teacher: nature. The toddler who climbs atop the piano and jumps to the floor quickly learns that laws are violated but not "broken." When he hits the floor, he is punished. Gravity "pays him back" for having violated its law, and he "pays" for having violated the law by hurting. He suffers the consequences of the violation.

We learned directly from our parents that wrongdoing deserves punishment. When the giants of our world seemed right in everything else, why should we have questioned their judgment? With rare exceptions we were soon agreeing, "My punishment is only what I deserve." When we learned that wrongdoing deserves punishment, it became a principle adopted for a lifetime.

Response to Anger by Retaliation

The need for payment by punishment also grows out of depression and anger with ourselves for having failed to live up to our own expectations. Hurt and anger seem to call forth a most primitive response -- attack in retaliation. When outraged, we say to ourselves in effect, "I'll pay you back for humiliating me. You will pay for hurting me!" The judgmental self that has been set up as an idol leers down from above as a god, accusing and demanding an atoning payment. The god must be placated. Only suffering will pacify that anger, at least for the time being.

Appeasement and Sacrifices

Whether the god is one's self or he bows to another, the response is much the same. Having violated his god's law, he feels the god is angered and may be expected to lash out in violent retribution. He reasons that if he does it to himself, maybe his god will not. Or he may feel that God is demanding a penance by which he is expected to punish himself as an atoning payment for his sin. Here is implied a further projection that God is saying, "If you do not punish yourself, I will, and my punishment of you will be far more severe than your own could ever be." This concept is so popular that a large segment of Christianity has institutionalized it as a regular practice. The atoning payment may take the form of any number of sacrifices. As we shall see in the pages to follow, the sacrifices may be offered in the form of the surrender of health, wealth, contentment, sanity, and even the last breath of life. Bear in mind that the "god" who is really making the demands for sacrifice is the deified self.

Almost every civilization has in its history a period in which sacrifices were made to its deity. When lesser offerings of grain, fruit, or the life of an animal were inadequate, a human life was sacrificed and offered in payment. If the life of a child seemed inadequate, that of a woman was offered. The ultimate offering was the life of the finest male specimen of human life available.

Archeologists have found sites where evidence points to the sacrificial offering of tens of thousands of human lives.

Most of us think of such primitive behavior as confined to the ancient past. In 1954, I clipped an article from the Far Eastern edition of the Stars and Stripes newspaper about a group in Cambodia who planned to sacrifice a child to the god of the Ton Lee Sap River, which was presumed to be angry because a bridge had been built across its waters. Although unlawful, hundreds in India are sacrificed each year, and anyone with access to the internet can go to Google, type the words "Muti killings" and find more than 500 articles describing sacrificial killings in modern Eastern Africa. Some of the followers of the Muti beliefs are believed to be responsible for human sacrifices each year even in modern London, England.

I once listened to a frightened teenage girl speak of the inner struggle she experienced when approached by members of a group with the suggestion that she give her life as a ritualized sacrifice in Satanic worship. I use the word struggle because of the appeal the idea had to her. The concept of making an atoning payment for violations of the accepted code of behavior seems to be almost as ancient as humankind and as modem as today.

Bartering with the Gods

Bargaining with the gods is not limited to efforts to appease – to lessen their anger. If one sacrifices something as a "gift to the gods," he may feel that he will get something in return. I have seen these "gifts" on numerous occasions during the years I lived and traveled throughout the Far East. A portion of fruit or grain was offered before enshrined, oddly shaped pieces of stone or coral, in hopes of receiving a safe trip on open seas in small canoes. (When one marvels at the sight of a small man returning from an overnight trip with a freshly-killed six-foot shark in the canoe with him, one suspects there has been assistance from somewhere!) He had made his offering to the "god of the sea." He returned, feeling that he had made a good trade. For his "payment to the god" he received a safe journey and food for his table as a bonus.

In a similar fashion, a modern man may attempt to make "trades" with his god in an effort to receive forgiveness. The payment may be in the form of a sacrifice of the best of his cattle, or by giving the best of his abilities for a period of time to help his neighbors in distress. Or one may make a sacrificial "payment by punishment," saying, "If I 'pay myself back' for my misdeeds, I can purchase my pardon." Though it may seem a rather crass observation, these "sacrifices" appear to be nothing less than profit motivated dealings with the divine, but as Dr. Paul Tournier, the noted French psychiatrist, insists, there is an ". . . idea deeply engraved in the heart of all men, that everything must be paid for" (p.174). Others suggest that the need to pay for wrongdoing is an innate characteristic of the human race.

Even the word "guilt" itself points to the concept of payment. It originates from the Anglo-Saxon word "gylt," meaning "to pay." The root word originally meant, "payment of a fine for an offense." In Yiddish, the word "gelt" means "money," a means of payment, and the German word for money is geld, closely related to our word "gold."

Evidence for the urge to make payment for misdeeds has been found on every continent and has been seen in almost every conceivable form. Millions of Hindus have enforced on themselves the suffering of miles of pilgrimage afoot, to plunge themselves in the Ganges River in efforts to wash away their sins. Others have broken and maimed their bodies in efforts to pay the price demanded in payment for their wrongdoing. I have watched as inch-square wafers of gold-leaf were placed on statues of Buddha by starving penitents, while the sweet fragrance of incense permeated the air. I have seen the products made of those sacrifices in the form of golden statues, ranging from a few inches in height to one that is more than a hundred feet long! Sacrificial payment is almost always from the most valued assets, ranging from the fattest of livestock to the healthiest of human bodies.

Payment by Flagellation

I once spent a pre-Easter day (Good Friday) in the town of Angeles, on the Philippine island of Luzon, observing a cult known as the "Flagellantes." I wanted to watch while they carried out their penitential rites of self-torture. Convinced that their load of guilt could be lifted only by subjecting themselves to the kind of suffering experienced by Christ on the day of His crucifixion, some had themselves tied to the crossbar of crosses made of green coconut logs. (When an experienced logger saw my photographs, he estimated that the logs weighed between 200 to 300 pounds.) Assistants pressed crowns made of thorns upon the heads of the penitents. As they struggled, dragging their crosses for several hours, friends walked beside them, adding pain by whipping their bare legs with switches.

Many others had numerous small cuts sliced into their backs with jagged glass. Then, as the blood oozed from the cuts, they began whipping themselves with a "cat-o'-nine-tails." Each applied his own whip. Swinging the whip back and forth, it wrapped around the body, flattening with a sickening "thump" against the back. Observers who ventured too close were splattered by the flying droplets of blood. The most vivid imagination will not likely picture the condition of those backs after several hours of continuous beating. The whips I saw had no objects in the ends of the tails of the "cats." But, newspapers later told of a group elsewhere on the same day that had fastened small nails and chips of glass into the ends of the whips. Some had actually had themselves nailed to the crosses. They had chosen their way of paying for their violations of their own adopted code of behavior.

Philip Yancey, in his book, *What's So Amazing about Grace,* told of Lakota warriors who "fastened eagle claws to their nipples and, straining against a rope attached to a sacred pole, fling themselves outward until the claws rip through their flesh. Then they enter a sweat lodge and pile high red-hot rocks until the temperature becomes unbearable, all in attempt to atone for sins" He went on to tell of having watched devout peasants with bloody knees crawl on cobblestone streets in Costa Rica and Hindus offer sacrifices to the gods of smallpox and poisonous snakes in India (p.34).

It has been said that a noted preacher of the previous century, the Rev. Dr. R. G. Lee, preached one particular sermon more than a thousand times. The title: "Payday Someday." It seems most appropriate that with the advance of age and experience, he received added acclaim by a new sermon: "Payday Everyday." When men choose to try to pay for their misdeeds, the payments get woven into the everyday fabric of life, as we will discuss in a short while.

Self-Punishment and Anxiety Reduction

We develop the practice of making "payment by punishment" from yet another source. When we were very young and did something wrong, we were punished. Keep in mind that a "punishment" may be as mild as a frown or as severe as the violent breaking of bones, and worse. We did something wrong; then we were punished. Similar experiences were repeated again and again and again. Each time we did something wrong, we were punished. One day we did something wrong – but the one who was expected to punish did not yet know about it. We waited, knowing that as soon as the "punisher" knew of our misdeed we would be punished. The anxiety of waiting and expecting seemed terrible! Finally, when we got the punishment, the misery of expectation was gone. We may have found, too, that the punishment was less severe than the anxious anticipation. After several experiences in which the pain of punishment was easier to endure than waiting for it, most of us concluded that punishment was preferable to waiting for it, and the sooner the better. This led to a decision, "I'll get someone to punish me or I will do it to myself"

The Curse of Damnation

It was many years ago, while still a college student, that I remember first seeing a man punish himself. As I stepped into the men's rest room, I saw a young man bent over a basin, washing his face. Raising his head and wiping his hands down across his face, he caught a glimpse of himself in the mirror. For a brief moment, the two faces exchanged glares of hatred. Then in rage he screamed, "You no good bastard! Damn you!" His fist lashed out, smashing into his own face in the mirror. Glass shattered and bones crunched against concrete blocks supporting the broken mirror. Surgeons spent hours trying to repair the damage. In a split second, his inner judge had pronounced the sentence and his inner executioner had begun meting it out.

There it is. The curse -- the curse of damnation -- the curse of destruction that hundreds of millions of human beings have passed on themselves -- the curse that is as old as humankind and as fresh as tomorrow's newspaper -- the curse that has brought as much death as all the wars of history, as much sickness as all the world's bacteria, and perhaps as much sorrow as all the world's deaths. This is the curse that begins with, "Damn you," in the mirror, and reaches out to "Damn you," across the dinner table and on to "Damn you," around the world.

With each conviction of guilt, the payment is made from the diminishing reserve of dignity and sense of personal worth. The self-dislike and anger against one's self mounts. The day-to-day violations slowly but surely deteriorate the character, eroding the whole personality.

Physical Self-Punishment
Self-executions
After repeated convictions of violation, there comes a time of crisis in which the inner judge loses patience with his criminal. In extreme instances, the internal judge may demand immediate execution.

Howard was taking his son to school after the boy had missed the bus. Somewhat angry and running late for an appointment of his own, the father swerved the pickup truck to enter the flow of traffic. The door flung open and the child was thrown out into the path of an oncoming car. The boy was killed instantly. Howard screamed out against himself for much of the afternoon. He cursed himself again and again as he paced the floor through most of the night. Just before dawn the next morning, he shot himself with a .45 caliber pistol. His "executioner" was quick and efficient.

The inner judge of a person with an overly scrupulous conscience may demand immediate execution for even minor infractions. The highly respected psychiatrist, Karl Menninger (p.336) tells of a twelve-year-old boy who hanged himself. In a note addressed to his parents, he confessed his motive. "I killed myself on account of me shooting a redbird. Good-bye, Mother and Daddy. I'll see you someday."

This self-imposed sentence of death was recognized as far back as the reign of Herodotus, about 425 BC. While on a hunt for wild boar, Adrastus hurled a spear that missed the boar but struck and killed the son of a dear friend. During the self-condemnation by Adrastus, the dead child's father is quoted as having said, "Enough my friend: I have all the revenge that I require, since thou givest sentence of death against thyself." The story continues by saying that as soon as all was quiet, Adrastus slew himself on the tomb of the dead child (tr. Tawlinson, p.15).

Suicide on the Installment Plan
We are fortunate that only a few of us have internal judges who are so insistent on immediate execution. Most executions are carried out on the installment plan. Without intervention, however, the end results will be

the same -- total destruction. Let's examine some of the slower, more subtle, but still common methods we tend to use to extract payment. Much of it is at a level somewhat below conscious intention. But the intention is there!

Recall that during such trials as those discussed in the foregoing chapter, the internal "defense council" offers one feeble defense after another in an effort to gain an acquittal. If the trial and expected verdict become too painful, we have the amazing capacity to bury it beneath the conscious memory. When the judgment of "guilty" is reached, and although we do not "hear" it, it is recorded, and in the subconscious level, we vaguely get the message. This experience of "forgetting" is the phenomenon commonly labeled "repression." This is not a conscious suppression of experience, "pushed" back out of the way with conscious intent. Rather, it becomes "lost" from consciousness and cannot be recalled at will. When any experience becomes too painful to endure, it may be completely removed from all the normal accesses of the memory. But it remains in that amazing memory-bank of the human brain. Our computers contain files of which we are totally unaware. Our brains also contain "files" we do not even remember having created.

Recall also that earlier we talked of the studies of Wilder Penfield, who pointed to evidence that nothing experienced is ever lost from healthy brain tissue. But under certain conditions the "lost" experience may resurface with vivid recollection of each detail and all accompanying feelings, or details of the event and feelings may emerge separately. For instance, there are occasions in which we may remember a dead loved one but feel no pain of sadness. At another time, we may suddenly feel sad for no apparent reason. A similar kind of separation can occur with a misdeed and its associated sense of guilt and shame. We may remember the act with no feelings at all. At another time we may feel only vaguely guilty for no apparent reason. More often we bypass both, not remembering the misdeed or the associated guilt and shame. We may feel only that we ought to be punished. This process may be compared to a decaying rat at the bottom of a pool. Though it is still far beneath the surface, enough unpleasant gases find their way to the top to keep reminding us that something unpleasant is down there.

Although the gases are making their way to the surface, the whole pool is becoming polluted in the process. It is becoming less and less a healthy place to live. The comparison is crude, but it has some parallels in the life of every human being.

Our lost, submerged, decaying feelings of guilt that cannot be remembered are still polluting. And they can pollute the whole body! This is commonly accepted as *fact* by the students of "psycho-physiologic disorders" in psychogenic (formerly called psycho-somatic) medicine. The feelings of guilt can and often do help produce physical illness. Guilt and other forms of stress are in the mainstream of any psychogenic (mind-body) study. Anything that has the power to distress the psyche has the power to distress the soma. That is, anything that has the power to distress the mind has the power to distress the body.

The ancient Greeks recognized the inter-connected, overlapping dimensions of that which makes up a whole person. Long before Christ, Socrates said that in order to understand and to treat the ills of man it was necessary to understand the whole of things in the person's life

(Weatherhead, p.106). The Greek word psyche has been variously translated in the New Testament and elsewhere as "soul," "being," "person," "personality," and "self." Common among some who provide modern medical care is the phrase, "holistic approach to patient care." The concern is for the physical-emotional-spiritual-social well-being of the patient.

This interrelatedness seems most easily understood when studied as it relates to anger. Bear in mind that a major part of our inner response to conviction of guilt is anger, anger toward ourselves for our misdeeds. Before you continue reading, pause a few moments and concentrate on your most recent experience of anger. Pick a time that you were most nearly in a rage. What happened to you physically?

I will mention the usual physical reactions as they come to mind, since I am aware of no significance to the order in which they may occur within us. When you became enraged, your body became tense. The muscle tone became more rigid, preparing you for battle. Your body has no way of differentiating an enemy "out there" from an enemy within. Not only might your hands have trembled but the palms of your hands and your armpits may have perspired quite freely. Someone may have suggested, "You shouldn't get your blood pressure up." Amid the anger, some blood vessels constricted and your heart beat faster. Other passageways may have opened wider, causing your face to turn red.

In effort to get more oxygen to the brain, your breathing became faster and shallower. The digestive system became stressed as the muscles in the stomach tightened. This tightening can be clearly measured under laboratory conditions. The saliva glands were so affected that your mouth became dry. Or these glands may have become quite overactive. The pupils of the eyes enlarged. As a part of this physical process, two small adrenal glands, located in the region of the kidneys, became overly active. Under extreme conditions the adrenal glands can become so excessively active they can spasm, bringing sharp, intense pain to the person in a sudden state of rage.

Only a moment of reflection will reveal that almost every system of the human body is brought into action in the experience of anger. Some are overworking. Others are under-working. This is the basis of all human illness. We become ill when, over an extended period of time, an organ becomes either overactive or under-active for any reason.

Try a simple experiment on yourself. Make a fist and hold it tight. One minute of this is sufficient to bring discomfort. Consider what would happen if the fist were maintained in that state of tension during a period that extended into weeks, months, or even years. Obviously, it would soon become a sick member of the body.

You may be saying, "But anger subsides." Yes, it does, if we are to remain healthy. But we tend to harbor grudges, often against ourselves! If the anger against ourselves originates from an ongoing state of guilt-feelings, our response may be buried in the pool of life's experiences and left to rot, just as the rat mentioned earlier. Though we may no longer remember the experience that produced the feelings of guilt, the guilt-feeling is there, keeping each of the systems of the body in a mild state of stress. The anger from the misdeed may be graphed approximately as indicated in figure 8.

Figure 8

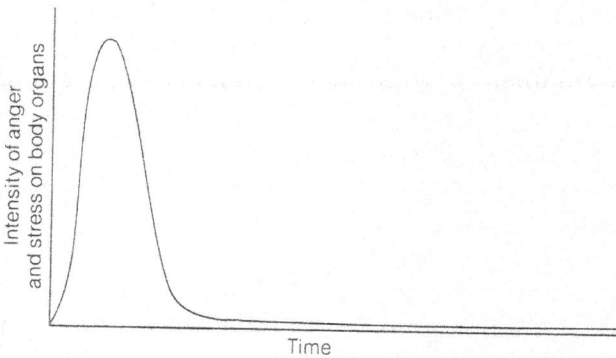

Each fresh experience of anger adds to the overall stress building within us. Add the feelings of greed, envy, anxiety, and excessive ambition. Each places its own portion of stress on various parts of the body, and, separately or combined, they have the capability of producing disease. This fact in no way denies the damage done by the invasion of bacteria or viruses. Rather, it points to the weakening of tissues and the upsetting of the balance of body chemistry by unhealthy emotions. There is ample evidence supporting the theory that these stresses create an instability that disturbs the necessary stable chemical ratio. This imbalance makes the body more susceptible to germs and viruses which normally would be resisted by natural barriers. Unless there is a source of relief, the stress mounts day after day, year after year.

Many years ago, a noted author of his period, Leslie Weatherhead, quoted the *British Medical Journal* as having said that no tissue of the human body is wholly removed from the influences such as these we are here discussing (Weatherhead, p.40). The most conservative estimates insist that at least half of the general hospital beds in the United States are filled with patients who have been made ill from emotionally originated sources

(Ashbrook, p.66). Many press the estimates above 85 percent. Call them "psychogenic" or "bad nerves," if you want. They are the same.

It is unfortunate that, in speaking of this process, some still refer to these illnesses as being "all in the mind." The layperson often concludes that he is being told that his illness is "imaginary." The patient naturally feels insulted. It's "for real" and he knows it! We have mounting evidence to support the belief that stresses damage immunizers that normally would protect the body. Whether the illness is in the form of a tension headache, a stomach ulcer, asthma, low back complications, heart disease, or any number of other illnesses, the sickness is real. The tissue damage, obvious to the trained eye, is often directly caused by inner stress involving damaged interpersonal relationships.

It must be accepted as a general truth: *sick relationships help produce sick bodies.* Whether the sick relationship is with one's friends, with his God, or with himself, this truth stands! As disease is often the body's way of crying, "You're guilty," the same is true of the accident. The intentional, though often unconscious, need to make one's self pay for a misdeed is at the root of the commonly recognized phenomenon of "accident proneness." One may pour out his entire cup of wrath upon himself, though he might never think of harming another. When 20 percent of the people have 80 percent of the accidents, something more than chance is working.

Purposeful Accidents
A study of automobile accidents has revealed that 4 percent of the drivers were involved in 36 percent of the accidents. One large trucking firm recognized that some drivers seemed to have repeated accidents. When

shifted to other types of work, these persons were found to have a high rate of accidents on the new job. It was also learned that these same persons had a high accident rate when away from work.

The intentional infliction of physical pain upon the self is one of the most common methods used to make one's self pay. It may be as openly and consciously intentional as the child who beat herself in the head with a hairbrush because she had "done bad things." Or it may be as unconsciously intentional as that which appears to be an "accident." It was Karl Menninger's study of "purposive accidents" in his classic, Man Against Himself (pp.318ff) that first piqued my interest in the power of unresolved guilt many years ago.

Harold dug a hole to bury an oil tank. He stepped to the other side of the house to talk with a neighbor. Returning to his work, he "wasn't watching" and fell into the open pit. Susan rolled up the carpet to have it cleaned. Having called the cleaner, she hung up the phone, turned, and stumbled over the carpet that she had "forgotten" about.

Though accidents are usually unconsciously intended, they are often calculated quite close to the surface of the mind. After his "accident," Alex was freely talking about some of his inner conflicts. As he talked of this injury, he suddenly remembered that an instant before he stepped into the path of an oncoming truck, he thought, "Here's what you deserve!" Wham!

Similar to the person who punishes himself with accidents is the one who punishes himself with sickness by agitating symptoms. Because of Sarah's diabetic condition, she was admitted to the hospital at least once a year to get her sugar-insulin balance regulated. She was normally limited to one small glass of her favorite fruit juice per day. But fully aware of the consequences, she occasionally felt the urge to drink two whole bottles of juice to get relief from "certain feelings way down inside." Examination of these "certain feelings" over numerous hours of counseling revealed them to be the feelings of guilt. After she paid her self-imposed penalty, her feelings of guilt were temporarily relieved. But self-imposed penalties never give lasting relief. After a period of time, the payment must be made again, somewhat like the promises of the blackmailer who promises, "just one more payment will be enough." Sarah learned to deal more constructively with her guilt, and she has gone for several years without having to be hospitalized for her diabetic problem.

Many people have been puzzled by the increase in numbers of people who continue to smoke years after the required health warning began to be printed on packages of cigarettes. When this law was passed, some of us predicted that for every person who stopped smoking because of the health hazard, another would begin for the simple fact that it is a health hazard. We were not wrong.

Purposeful Obesity
Most people realize that excessive weight is harmful to health. I maintain that a large percentage of those who are overweight are intentionally trying to harm themselves. As one person said, "I hate me so much I just want to bury me alive in fat." Carrying more than 300 pounds, Marie, responding to her guilt, would eat three pies at a sitting and then look into the mirror and say, "Now die, damn you, die!" (Of course, there are other motives for obesity but they are irrelevant to this discussion.)

Substance Abuse

Narcotics are used effectively at times by the internal "defense counsel" to silence the sound of the inner accusing voice. But they also are used by the internal "executioner" in an effort to make one's self pay for the misdeeds for which there has been a conviction. This is but one of the strongest attractions for the drug abuser.

A young man with a brilliant mind sat on his hospital bed discussing his use of heroin. I asked, 'Why? Why are you doing this to yourself? It seems useless for me to tell you the damage you are doing to yourself. You probably know more about it than I do. I suspect there is a reason and that you know it. Do you object to telling me?" Without a moment of hesitation he responded, "Chaplain, you ought to know the answer to that question without me telling you. Sure, I know. I feel so bad about some of the things I've done, I want to die. I don't have the guts to pick up a gun and blow my brains out, so I just do it the slow way with drugs. I feel like I've have to pay for what all I've done wrong. I think that most of us who are using this stuff feel the same way." How much more clearly could he have spelled it out? He was killing himself -- committing suicide on the installment plan in an effort to punish himself!

While on the subject of drugs, it is necessary to include the use of alcohol as a method of self-punishment. In response to an inner condemning voice, a man may turn to the bottle. He may then condemn himself for having become intoxicated. He again turns to the bottle to silence the accuser and to make himself pay. This becomes an endless cycle as the alcoholic spirals downward to destruction.

Workaholism
Another method of punishing oneself is by overwork. In the early 1970s, the Rev. Dr. Wayne Oates introduced a new word into our vocabulary, "Workaholism." In his Confessions of a Workaholic (p.5), he pointed to work as a means of punishing one's self for misbehavior. In effect, the victim is saying, "anyone who has done (or thought or felt) as I have, deserves little rest. I deserve weariness. I have, because of my behavior, forfeited the right to a rested mind and body."

Become Imprisoned
Those studying human behavior in response to guilt feelings have long been convinced that a high percentage of prison inmates performed their violations of law in order to get themselves punished.

In a fit of violent anger, Jack killed his wife. No one was surprised when he was sent to the state prison. After several years, Jack learned he was scheduled for parole, but two weeks before the date of his release, he escaped. Two nights later, he was arrested after having broken into a supermarket less than a mile from the prison. It was late at night. The lights were on. He was seen walking around inside, having left the doors standing wide open on a busy street. The expertise of the prison psychologists was not required to interpret Jack's behavior. Back in his home community, ordinary working people, with no more than a high school education concluded that Jack felt that he had not yet been adequately punished for his crime.

Consider the experience of a man with whom I became quite well acquainted. Tom carried a pistol while he burglarized a store. He heard a noise and glanced around to see a policeman coming through the door with his pistol drawn. Tom later remembered a fleeting thought, "I don't deserve to live. I can get him to kill me." He wheeled around, pulling his gun from his belt. The policeman fired first. Surgeons removed the bullet from Tom's chest, and the judge removed Tom from society. Tom went to prison.

Those drafting state laws on the death penalty should give careful consideration to this all-too-common need of men to have themselves punished. When death becomes a promised blessing for someone, a capital crime may be carried out in hope of getting the death sentence. The criminal says, in essence, "If I violate the law, I can get someone to punish me," This seems evidenced in statistics presented by Henry Weihoten, who was honored back in the mid-1950s by the American Psychiatric Association for his contributions in psychology and law. He stated in his book, The Urge to Punish (p.147):

Of the eight states having the lowest murder rate in the United States, five have no death penalty. The state with the very lowest murder rate is Maine which abolished capital punishment in 1870. The state with the highest murder rate is Georgia. It is also the state that itself does more killing than any other, with 280 executions in twenty years as against 270 for the four times more populous New York, and 124 for the three times more populous state of Pennsylvania.

Brian Forst, a senior research analyst with the University of Minnesota Institute of Law and Social Research, published basically the same conclusion back in the Fall 1977 University of Minnesota *Law Review*. Forst's conclusions followed a careful review of the murder statistics for thirty-two states between 1960 and 1970.

While it is popularly assumed that capital punishment is a deterrent to murder, statistical evidence is mounting to support the idea that the possibility of a death sentence may indeed promote murder instead of deterring it (Walt Menninger, pp.5-7). It does happen. Gordon Powell tells the following story:

In June, 1958, the Massachusetts Supreme Court was thrown into turmoil when a clean-cut, pink-cheeked, twenty-one-year old man named Jack Chester not only pleaded guilty to the charge of murdering a young lady, but insisted that no mercy be shown to him, and he be sentenced to die in the electric chair as soon as possible. Young Chester had gone to the Boston home of his girlfriend, Beatrice Fishman, and shot nine bullets through a flimsy door to kill her. His mother retained the services of the best lawyer she could get to defend her son and they fought a tremendous battle, but they could not prevent him from going to the stand and saying to the jury, "I'm not denying the fact that what I did to Beatrice Fishman was premeditated, cold-blooded murder. It is my opinion that any decision other than guilty -- guilty of murder in the first degree, with no recommendation for leniency is a miscarriage of justice."

The jury, hardly able to believe their ears, condemned him to death as he requested. The explanation was given by psychiatrists who said that fifteen years before, when Jack Chester was a small boy of six, he had gone out on a cold day without his hat, in spite of his mother's efforts. His father had followed him with the hat, but, apparently slipping on some ice, he fell and received such injuries that he died a month later. The boy always believed that he was responsible for his father's death. His feelings of guilt grew so strong that he made several attempts to take his own life.

He also developed fantasies that he would die young. Obsession with his guilt produced a compulsion in him which became a death wish. He had to do something to bring about his punishment by death (Powell p.26f).

Going without punishment may be a more severe form of suffering than the actual punishment; this is a truth long recognized. In the dialogues of Plato titled "Gorgias," Socrates is quoted as saying, "Let us investigate the second point at issue between us, whether as you thought to be punished when guilty is the greatest of evils or, as I thought, it is a greater evil to escape punishment" (Plato, p.258). There is ample evidence that this is a conclusion reached by almost every person. It is a conclusion that may not be reasoned out, but yet dwells within the deeper recesses at the level of feeling.

Emotional Tools of Torture
The emphasis up to this point has been on physical punishment. Of course, emotional pain is affiliated with each of them. Other "tools of torture" available for use by our inner "executioner" are more directly emotional. The two are separated only for the purpose of discussion. "Make him pay!" is still the cry of the inner judge and jury. In speaking of childhood, I have often heard some say they would have preferred a spanking than to be scolded by their parents. "The scolding seemed to hurt more." When the physical punishment was over, the sting goes away and is soon forgotten, but the echoes of the scolding come again and again, bringing back pain with each memory.

Coincidental to the writing of these paragraphs about punishing ourselves by inflicting emotional pain, I was listening to a young man wrestle with the feeling that he was somehow responsible for his brother's misbehavior. He concluded that, in reality, his brother was responsible for his own behavior. He added that someone would get hurt by trying to force his brother to do anything against his will. He showed insight as he concluded: "While I have been accepting responsibility for his behavior, I have been miserable! I've been punishing myself for my own misbehavior." This was his conclusion; in no way had I suggested it. He had no way of knowing I had written the foregoing paragraphs early that morning. He went on to say he had the feeling that if he stopped punishing himself in this manner, he would find another punishment to take its place. There is, indeed, that danger.

It should be noted here that there is a compounding pattern in all forms of self-punishment. This is necessary, since the amount of pain inflicted is rarely enough. The inner judge keeps crying, "More! More!" One can never pay enough for his own misdeeds. The relief is temporary at best.

Forced Rejection

Rejection is the price men often pay for their sense of guilt. Most of us have known people who drive away those who love them. As love is offered, they will "bite the hand that feeds them." To a caring gesture, they respond with an insult. If the one making the caring overture withdraws, the response is, "I knew it. Nobody loves me. If he really cared about me, he would have tolerated all my ill manners and insults." No matter how often love is extended, the same thing happens. Each rejection provides the pain that gives temporary satisfaction. "Hurt me more! Give me what I deserve. I don't deserve your affection." Recently a young man, engulfed in tears, confided, "I've run off everybody who has tried to love me. I know I don't deserve anybody's love."

By this time, I hope you recognize that I am not writing about my own or someone else's theological/ psychological theory. I am forced to write on the basis of that which I watched and heard during more than forty-five years at the bedside of my patients and behind the closed doors of my counseling office.

Surrender of Sanity

As one's screaming judge cries louder and louder for payment, some seek to escape, but ironically, some pay with their very sanity. Behind virtually every psychosis lays some extreme sense of guilt and shame. Knowing the place of chemical imbalances in mental illness, I am growing in the suspicion that the inner stress created by the sense of guilt is helping to create the chemical imbalances. We have to look no farther than the tear glands to see that emotions stimulate secretions from glands.

One expression of a psychosis is a break with reality in which one sees himself as someone great. Dr. Milton Rokeach, a psychologist, tells of a study of three such persons in his book, *The Three Christs of Ypsilanti*. He placed three patients, all of whom claimed to be Jesus Christ, in the same ward. After many months together, one began to show some improvement, whereupon he changed his name from Jesus Christ to Dung. About this patient, Rokeach wrote:

The dominant theme is not shame about incompetence but guilt about forbidden sexual and aggressive impulses. Leon is a guilt-ridden Christ who strives more to be good than great: he is suffering not so much from a delusion of greatness as from a delusion of goodness (p.114).

In his flight from the scream of "guilty" by his inner judge, Leon had to become one in which there was no wrong. To escape seeing himself as the "filthiest" of things, he had to go all the way in the opposite direction, seeing himself as the purest of persons. Neither view of himself was realistic, but it was a price paid for the violation of his sense of "oughtness." What everyone pays in small amounts, Leon paid in near-total – his sense of dignity, worth, and ultimately his sanity.

And there is yet another consequence. The psychotic patient usually feels a strong sense of guilt for being different enough to be in a mental hospital. He is failing to be as he "ought." Dr. Ernest E. Brewder, having ministered for many years as a chaplain in a mental hospital wrote, "We believe . . . that mentally ill patients come to feel they ought to be punished, ought to be ostracized and do belong in such a place of known stigma as the mental hospital" (p.33).

Perpetual Discontent
One type of self-punishment that must be noted might be titled "perpetual dissatisfaction." Using this form of self-torture, the guilty person sees himself as undeserving of contentment – deserving only discontentment. Behaving as he has, he feels he deserves the misery of discontent. Therefore, he may be looking always to the horizon for a grand and glorious tomorrow, refusing to accept the joys of today. Or he may always look over his shoulder to the times when everything was better than it is now. Yesterday was always better than today.

Each decision seems to be unconsciously designed to make him more miserable so that he can look with dissatisfaction with what he has at the moment. A man, dissatisfied with his old job, accepts a new one, but then decides the previous job was better than what he now has. A man wants out of what he believes to be a bad marriage. When the marriage dissolves, he looks back to the beautiful marriage he has deserted. When remarried, he looks back, remembering the joys of having lived as a bachelor.

He seems to pervert the writing of the Apostle Paul, who said he had determined to be content in whatever state he found himself (cf. Phil. 4:11). (Keep in mind that Paul was writing from a filthy ancient Roman prison.) The person who needs to punish himself has determined that in whatever state he finds himself, he shall be discontent. Happiness to him is somewhat like the elusive butterfly; it is always where he has just been but he did not recognize it nor really possess it when it was there.

Legal Anxiety

One man confided that after listening to one of my lectures on this subject, added thought had forced him to conclude that he was writing bad checks as a way of punishing himself. Keeping himself in a state of anxiety over the outcome, he was making himself pay for previous misbehavior.

Financial Anxiety

Others keep themselves economically drained because they feel they do not deserve economic comfort. They are saying, in effect, "Anyone who has done as I have, deserves to stay in an economic bind."

"Give Us Hell"

I have long been fascinated by the praise given to gospel ministers who condemn, "step on toes," and "peel hide." I've been invited on numerous occasions by church lay leaders to come and "Really let us have it." "Pour it on." One urged, "Preach at us so hard that we'll feel the flames of hell." Those who have a need to be hurt by the pain of fear, anxiety, and reminders of their worthlessness find joy in their suffering. They have, for the moment, paid the price. And the obliging minister has helped them to atone!

Let's Keep the Marriage Miserable

Many years ago, while my wife and I were in our theological seminary studies, we became interested in the problem of alcoholism. For many months we listened and became part of almost all the activities within the local chapter of an alcoholic rehabilitation program. I became such a part of the program that some of the men threatened, in jest, to take me out and get me drunk so that they could make me a member of their organization. During that time, I discovered a major problem in family adjustment.

If a man was destroying himself with alcohol, his wife usually was miserable. She worried about him. He often verbally assaulted her to the point of tears, and sometimes the assault was physical. Through declining health and into economic poverty, she stayed with him. After years of misery for both, one day he quit the bottle. Though she would tell of the marvelous improvements in his life, with few exceptions the wife's dissatisfaction increased and the marriage deteriorated more rapidly.

My wife brought to my attention one of the most important elements in such marital breakdowns:

"These women are missing something. They are no longer getting what they need. They need an over-sized bottle-baby to look after. They use the husband's drinking problem to satisfy their own need to be abused, and to fulfill an unending mothering role. Being unhappy has been satisfying to them, and although they now continue to be unhappy, it is for a different reason. They no longer receive the treatment they feel they deserve."

Now, many years later, I am convinced we all elicit from people the kind of treatment we feel we deserve, whether good or bad. Indeed, we demand it! When others fail to meet our often unspoken demands, the relationship deteriorates.

Marriage for Misery
During forty-five years of marriage counseling, I listened to couples as they retrace the history of their marital discord. In my earlier years, I was astonished at how many people had a sick relationship long before the marriage ceremony. They have quietly said to themselves, "This is the kind of person who will help me to stay as miserable as I feel I deserve." It appears that the need for punishment by persons suffering from guilt may be the motivation for as many marriage ceremonies as love, and, unfortunately, this need for punishment is often misidentified as "love." It is difficult to conclude otherwise when I consider the many times I've heard such comments as, "I don't know why I love him so desperately. I have black-and-blue marks from where he hits me. I know he goes out with other women all the time, but I just can't bear the thought of life without him." She means that she is in "love" with the misery he helps her to feel, and that she cannot bear the thought of life without his pain-inflicting personality.

Reflecting casually on his past, a man rather matter-of-factly observed, "Mother felt so guilty about the way she treated Daddy that, after he died, she married a weak, ineffectual drunk. She wouldn't divorce. That would be against her 'religion.' But we all knew that she really felt she now had what she deserved."

Julie sat with her head down, apparently trying to conceal her black eye. The large dark-blue splotch on her right arm looked newer than the yellowish-green bruise on her shoulder. Her husband tried to explain. "Chaplain, I've tried to stop beating her, but she won't let me. Several months ago, I tried to stop. I know a guy shouldn't beat up on his wife. I decided that no matter what happened I wouldn't hit her. Do you know what she did? She belted me on the side of my head with a frying pan. When I still didn't hit her, she got right up to my face and stood there screaming. I suddenly knew what she wanted. I stepped back and slapped hell out of her, and she calmed down immediately. She wanted to make love a few minutes later!"

For better or for worse, two people choose each other as partners to help them to be as happy or as unhappy as they feel they deserve! Coming out of a marriage by way of divorce, people often have a feeling of relief. "Finally! I'm away from that 'so and so' who has made me miserable." Unfortunately, this person is in danger of becoming married again to someone with traits almost identical to those of the former marriage partner. The thing so despised about the first partner may be the very trait that drew them together and is potentially the trait that is drawing them toward a second marriage. This attraction is misinterpreted, and people dignify it by calling it "love."

Emerging from marriage failure almost always leaves both parties with a sense of guilt. This will be true even of the one most "innocent." Who can endure failure without some sense of guilt? Not many. But are we not already thinking about failure -- failure to live up to an "ought."

Cycle of the Damned

Close to half of this chapter has dealt with forms of failure that has been used as methods of payment by punishment. These were payments, however, that resulted in additional failure! There is always the resultant feeling, "I ought not to have failed!" We saw how failure to live up to one's sense of "ought" led to self-induced failure of health. Another failure led to the self-induced failure to maintain economic security. Other failures led to the need to punish with self-induced insanity. We saw that others, having failed to live up to some sense of "oughtness," made themselves pay by inducing failure to be content. Now we have observed that many, failing to live up to some former "ought," have worked to create failure in their marriages.

We are looking into the face of one of the most terrible realities experienced by humankind: For every failure to live up to some "ought," there is the tendency to punish one's self in such a manner as to produce another failure! And every failure produces the response, "I ought not to have failed!" I stand convicted of having violated an 'ought' that in turn produces the need for further punishment which results in further failure. Having failed, I punish myself in such a manner as to produce a further sense of failure. A cycle is complete, only to begin again: I have failed to live up to an 'ought,' for which I feel guilty. Convicted of guilt I feel the need to pay. To pay, I choose a method that will leave me with

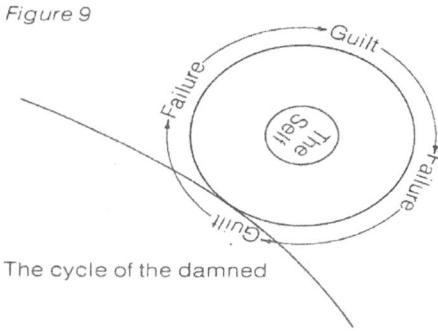

Figure 9

The cycle of the damned

a sense of having failed. (See figure 9)

The cycle once more completed, it begins again. On and on rolls the cycle downward. It may be compared to a snowball rolling down hill, adding to its load and momentum with each revolution. The load of guilt that is picked up becomes greater and greater, and the rate of descent becomes faster and faster. This "cycle of the damned" goes round and round and down and down and has the potential of going on and on eternally. That is at least one aspect of hell!

Addictions
Look at this cycle in some of the more obvious examples. One of the easiest to observe is alcoholism. This cycle must be considered as one of the major contributing factors to the problem of alcohol addiction. Note how one man expressed it. "I don't remember why I got drunk to start with, but after I did, I felt so disgusted with myself I got drunk again. I guess I get drunk now because I get drunk. I hate the sight of me. How can you stand to look at me?"

The same cycle is functioning in "foodaholism" and must be regarded as a major contributing factor to obesity. A part of the "hunger" is the insatiable appetite for punishment. It has been summed up by, "I eat too much because I feel guilty, and then because I feel guilty I eat too much." Another said, "Because of some of the things I've done, I feel I need to be punished. I punish myself by overeating. Then I hate myself more for eating so much so I feel like I need to be punished. Then I punish me by overeating and on and on I go!" The results were obvious. This woman put into words her own version of the cycle of the damned.

Flight from Freedom – Addiction to Self-Destruction

Recognizing that some addictions become physical dependencies, I still suspect that, with few exceptions, the "cycle of the damned" is a continuing part of every addiction; therefore, I suggest that the basic addiction is an addiction to self-destruction. I can find no basis to debate against those who tell us that the addiction ultimately is an addiction to sin.

We see pure irony here. Bound by the insatiable need to pay for previous misbehavior by self-degrading, self-defeating behavior, the person is likely to boast of his freedom. "Don't try to restrict me with rules of behavior. I'm free and I'll do as I please." With few exceptions, it takes little observation to see that the person making such a statement is already up to his waist in his quicksand-like efforts at self-atonement. He is locked in slavery by his own passions. His "freedom" is his slavery. (During the Second World War, Erich Fromm wrote a whole book, *Escape from Freedom,* about this phenomenon. I have seen nothing on the subject that surpasses it in quality. See Bibliography.)

Their adjustment to bondage in misery becomes so fully accepted that potential freedom presents an anxious threat. Edward Stein, in *Beyond Guilt,* tells of Warden Duffy's experience with a prisoner of San Quentin Prison. The man was in his seventies. It was time to release him. For many years, he had yearned for freedom, but when the time came for his release, he begged Duffey to let him stay in prison. He no longer had a family. He had no way to support himself, and he had no place to go. He said, "I'm too old to start over. This is the only life I know." They let him stay. He had an unlocked cell and could come and go at will within the prison.

Warden Duffy said, "One day, as a kindness, I offered to take him out for an automobile ride to see how the world had changed during his stay in prison. He was actually fearful, and refused, saying, 'Oh, no, you'll get me out there and turn me loose, then won't let me back in!' " (Stein, p.49).

It becomes the task of the family, the friend, the minister, the psychiatrist, the church, and the entire helping, caring community to create a climate and vision of something valuable, desirable, and enviable to attract the "prisoner" to life outside the cycle of the damned. Only if a person recognizes his potential future as totally devastating and decides that he wants something better for himself will he ever be set free. The Apostle Paul wrote, "You belong to the power which you choose to obey, whether you choose sin, whose regard is death, or God, obedience to whom means the reward of righteousness" (Rom. 6:16 Phillips Trans.). Paul was writing of those caught in the cycle of the damned.

Usually blind to their bondage and finally sinking in the quicksand of self-destruction, their last words may be, "I'm really living it up." This is no exaggeration. As a hospital chaplain, I've seen their bodies brought into the emergency room, dead on arrival. Their peers shake their heads in disbelief. Their families shed tears in grief. Some have muttered, "At least, he died happy." They were happy to be living a destructive lifestyle. They have died in the misery they have invited – even forced into their own lives.

The death may be the result of an accident, disease, or conscious suicide. "The wages of sin is death" (Rom. 6:23). I've seen it too many dozens of times. One young man left behind a typical suicide note. "To everyone I love. All I brought into the world is sorrow and pain. God gave me life, but I do not deserve it." The note was found by his body after he shot himself. We give ourselves the kind of treatment we feel we deserve.

More Self-defeat

Let's move on before the reader concludes that the "cycle of the damned" relates only to the addicted. How does this cycle relate to the lives of those who are more "normal"? We combine many varied elements into the different rotations of the cycle.

Gene seduced one of the girls at his office, for which he later felt guilty. To punish himself, he openly confessed to his wife. Seeing how hurt she was, he felt guilty again. To punish himself he unconsciously turned off the alarm clock, making himself quite late for an important meeting with a client who was thereby insulted. Feeling guilty for the resultant failure to get the contract, he concluded he didn't deserve such a good job. When he was fired, friends could not understand why one as intelligent as he would misuse the company credit card. "Surely he didn't think he could get away with that?" No, he didn't. Just beneath the surface of his conscious mind he had "planned" his punishment one step at a time, each step an atoning payment for the preceding steps! Of course this is not the end. "Sin, when it is full-grown, gives birth to death" (James 1:15 TEV). He now felt the need to punish himself for his theft. We need not continue with his story. After all, we see it lived out all around us almost every day.

Note that each step involved a failure. He failed morally with the girl. He failed in his commitments to his wife. He failed to get out of bed, which set himself up to fail at his job. Then he failed the trust placed in him by his employer. We looked at only a few steps along his way down. The cycle did not begin with his affair with the office girl, nor did it end with being fired from his job. Each failure was an atoning payment for the failure before! One such person, bound within this cycle, tearfully observed, "I feel like I'm in a deep hole trying to dig my way out; but instead of coming any nearer to the top of my well, I find that I'm just getting deeper." Another said, "I'm so tired of this kind of life, but I feel like I'm in chains that are dragging me to the depths of the lowest hell."

The sense of wrong does not have to be associated with any specific deed; it may be an un-definable feeling toward the past. "Just as anxiety (as contrasted to *fear*) does not have an object, guilt likewise is often experienced as a vague and diffuse sense of value loss, without being tied to identifiable times and places" (Oden, p.74) Whether vague or specific, guilt demands punishment.

Academic failures, moral failures, economic failures, pro-fessional failures, social failures, and marital failures are among the failures our internal "executioner" tends to use as a scourge each time the internal judge says, "Guilty!"

The "Death-instinct"

Sigmund Freud often has been scorned for his theory of the "death-instinct," even though he spoke also of the "life-instinct." He saw two forces in conflict and simply wrote of what he saw. Much earlier, the Apostle Paul observed what appears to be the same two forces of conflict even in himself, and he wrote of what he saw. Recorded in the New Testament, he said that though he delights in the "law of God," he could see within himself "another law" which he called "the law of sin" (Rom. 7:23-25). One of these forces pulled him toward life as the other pulled him toward death. One pulled him toward constructive modes of behavior while the other pulled toward the destructive.

Back to the Law of Mortigression

Throughout this chapter, we have been observing the law of mortigression in action. It is similar in statement to the physical law of momentum. Let's look at it again: "A personality in the process of deterioration tends to continue in the process of deterioration unless acted on by an outside force." That deterioration has been seen to operate by two separate processes. The first was erosion -- that process of moral decay and personality disintegration which has no relation to any feeling of guilt.

This process is at work in every "wrong" act (that's one reason it's wrong) and is most observable in the "sociopath," that rapidly-deteriorated personality who has no recognizable feeling of guilt or wrongdoing.

Though we may not fully know why he has no sense of guilt for even the most hideous of crimes, we can see why he degenerates. Disintegration is the natural consequence of wrong behavior, just as falling is the natural consequence of jumping from the fifteenth floor of a building. "A man reaps what he sows" (Gal. 6:7 NEB).

The "law of mortigression" was next seen active in the vicious "cycle of the damned." With each conviction for failure, the inner judge demanded payment which the self paid with still another failure! The consequences of both of these are disastrous.

There is a truth that must be understood. Read the next lengthy sentence ten times if necessary to understand it. *If there were no God to be affronted, no Bible or other religious writing to obey or disobey, nor any other religious influence in our lives, then greed, envy, laziness, gluttony, undisciplined expression of sexual need, unharnessed anger, and conceitful pride would still produce essentially the same eroding, dehumanizing, damning results as they do now!* And this included only the classic seven listed as "deadly sins" over fifteen-hundred years ago (Whitlow, p.22.) Personality-eroding behavior erodes without regard to one's "religious" or "nonreligious" standards.

The alarming question has been repeatedly asked: "Is there no stopping the process of disintegration?" Is there no salvation from these ongoing consequences?" There is indeed! And we will deal with that in the final chapter, but first we need to pause, step back, and try to see all of this in perspective. Any effort to graphically portray the course of a human life has its limitations. However, figure 10 is an attempt to illustrate the tragedy of past, present, and future as it relates to the foregoing pages.

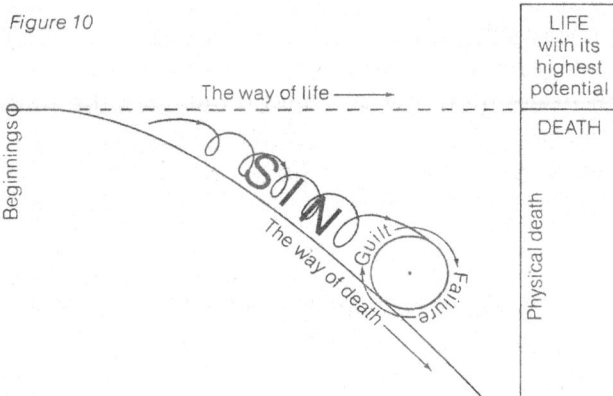

Figure 10

Since the departure from the original course to life with its highest potential, there has been a steady erosion of the personality moving farther and farther away from life. The personality is in the process of destruction. His humanity is dying! Just as the time-span between birth and death varies with each person, so does the rate of descent. (In figure 10, the downward sloping curved line represents this rate of descent.)

Caught in the "cycle of the damned," the farther one goes, the more rapid his descent and, like the snowball gathering momentum, the harder it is to stop one from totally destroying himself. (Remember the law of mortigression.) Not only is the person caught up in the need to destroy himself, but, almost invariably, he feels the need to take others down with him. He seems to want company on his journey toward destruction. He will not only encourage his companions to indulge in the same type of behavior, he will also lure "innocent" parties he meets along the way. When he reflects on his misbehavior, his curse of, "I'll be damned," is not as much a profane expression of amazement as it is an additional curse he declares against himself.

Unfortunately, sin is usually thought of as being a particular act. This limited view of sin loses sight of the fact that sin is also a verb: a process or pattern of behavior and attitude. It is that way of life vividly seen in the "cycle of the damned!" It is a lifestyle -- a "way of life," however, that is most accurately and appropriately described as a "way of death" – that which St. Augustine called the murder of one's own "real human being." (Pusey, p.27)

Hell This Side of the Grave

Hopefully, such a person will become frightened. "If I keep going as I am now, I have a hell of a future ahead." The profane language is often quite graphic and precise. Its meaning is exact. He is, indeed, facing a "hell of a future." It is a hell to which he has damned himself and for which men commonly blame God. It is the result of one's own consignment. His "hell" only begins on this side of the grave. I have often listened to those in the process of self-destruction, caught and being pulled down by the forces of hatred, greed, envy, and lust. Their current distress is already "hellacious." They are already in a hell they have created for themselves by their pattern of life. Hell begins on this side of the grave!

As a boy, each winter I helped in the killing, cleaning, and dressing of hogs. The part I especially disliked was the sight of the involuntary muscle contractions as the dying animal jerked again and again until it was finally dead. I've also watched men die with the same kind of convulsive muscular contractions. It is the process of dying that is always vaguely sickening and sad to me.

Although I haven't been around at "hog-killing time" for many years, I still get that same nauseous feeling as I observe people caught up in their self-defeating, self-destroying, self-damning behavior. I've watched an alcoholic raise a glass to his lips, and I've thought, "This is his process of dying. These movements are somewhat similar to the involuntary muscular contraction of something or someone dying." His words and behavior reveal that he's already suffering in the flames of his hell.

On Bourbon Street, in New Orleans, I heard a hawker at the door to a strip show yell, "Come on in and see the nude girls on stage. They hide nothing." I thought, "He's inviting me to watch young women in their agonizing process of dying, and he wants me to pay money to encourage them to hasten the process!" Their contortions are the veiled motions of women writhing in the agonizing pain of their own private hell, which stems from their hatred of themselves! In their occasional moments of honesty, I've listened to those caught up in degrading, dehumanizing, demoralizing behavior which results in further self-hatred and disgust. Their words convey pain. Their feelings convey suffering. I have felt the hurt as it passed to me empathically. They are already feeling the early pains of hell.

As opposed to the concept of God as characterized by the famous sermon of Jonathan Edwards, Sinners in the Hands of an Angry God, Christianity has often turned from the idea that Jehovah can ever become angry or wrathful because of the behavior of mortals. There is no question that the Holy Scriptures teach that God is love. There is, however, ample evidence from the same sacred writings that points to the fact that there are times in which Jehovah becomes wrathful against the extremely harmful behavior of His creatures.

Is it contradictory to speak of Him as being loving and angry at the same moment? It may be that because He is capable of such deep love that He may become angrily distressed with human behavior.

Consider the family whose home was overrun by enemy troops advancing in war. The father was bound hand and foot and suffered the agony of watching his wife and children molested and then butchered. Can we imagine that husband and father having been less than enraged at the mistreatment of those he loved? These were not men against whom he felt enraged. They had lost their humanity. They had become animals! Or had these creatures become something even less than animals? God loves the human race. Can He refrain from becoming irate as He watches those who have become so deteriorated that their behavior is less than animal-like? Would not any loving father become enraged as he watched his children suffer abuse at the hands of brutes?

God the Father sees His children abused daily. It is because He loves humankind that He may become angry and possibly wrathful. It seems possible that God's wrath may be most terribly expressed by passively allowing the disobedient, disintegrating personality to continue his or her destructive route to continue beyond the grave.

Wait! There is an alternative!
However, before we go there, we must look at another issue that is just as destructive. Recall that while we are on trial in our own inner courtroom, a part of our fragmented personality is a Defense Counselor who has the job of trying to get a judgment of "Not Guilty." Cursed

is the person who has a highly successful inner Defense Counselor. If he/she is too effective, the conscience can be eliminated.

Some Experience Little or No Sense of Guilt Feelings

From the earliest days that I began seriously studying issues related to guilt, friends and acquaintances repeated asked one question, "Why are you planning to write a book about guilt? Nobody feels guilty for anything any more." That statement recognizes one end of a spectrum. People's response to wrong behavior falls somewhere along a continuum between "none" and "deadly." One person can spit on the sidewalk and feel guilty for it ten years later. Another may rape and dismember a six-year-old child and feel no pangs of remorse whatsoever. We have examined those who feel intensely guilty. Now, we must look at those who experience little or no feeling of guilt.

Back in the early 1970s, the renowned Psychiatrist, Dr. Karl Menninger, raised the question, in his book, *Whatever Became of Sin.* It was obvious to those who read the answer to his question, that he was convinced that *sin* is still with us despite the unpopularity of the word. If somebody has "sinned," as Menninger insists, somebody is guilty. But whatever became of guilt? We don't like the word.

The "Not Me" spirit haunts almost every family! (It's real name may be "Not I," but it is better known among most folks as "not me.") The top is left off the stick of glue. Wet leaves from someone's shoes litter the living room carpet. The front door is left open in the middle of winter. Ask every member of the family and no one admits having made the mistake. The "not me" spirit has invaded the home. On the construction site, one corner of the concrete foundation of the new apartment building is five inches too high. Ask the fourteen men on the job who was responsible and every one of them can tell you, "It was '"not me."' The job superintendent was almost sure before he asked. He knew by experience. This mischievous spirit seems to be everywhere! It's in homes, in industry, and in every level of government. If the problem involved only trivialities, we might be able to "laugh it off" as we might when watching the antics of "Casper the Friendly Ghost" during the Saturday morning cartoon hour.

But the consequences are dire, and nothing is amusing about the tragedies for which no one accepts the blame. Indeed, many have been taught by renowned scholars that "no one is ever to 'blame.' No one is ever really 'responsible'." (Ellis, pp.133 & 137) When no one is responsible, the atrocities go on. From the word "atrocities," it is obvious that we are approaching issues bigger than wet leaves on the living room carpet or a few inches of concrete that can be cut away. Such matters are as personal as a man destroying himself with alcohol, as international as a power-hungry government forcibly taking control of its neighbor, and as global as a world poisoning itself with its own waste products.

Listen to those involved. Hear the typical responses. Who is responsible for the pollution of the once-pure streams of the world? "Not me" says each of those boating off down the lake, strewing trash and garbage in their wake. "My little bit is not enough to count. It's the big industrial plants that are making our waters so filthy."

"Not me," says the industrialist, "I'm just providing jobs and putting out a product at the lowest price I can to make a profit for the stockholders and to help keep down inflation. Other means of disposing of industrial wastes would only drive up the prices. Besides, everybody else is doing it, and if you want the truth, the real polluters are the large cities who are dumping raw sewage into the streams."

"Not me," says the city mayor. "We are just trying to keep down taxes that would surely have to be raised if we were to build adequate sewage treatment and disposal plants. The culprits are really the individual taxpayers who howl every time we propose some new project." The projected "blame" has gone full circle with everyone pointing to someone else, and they forget to mention the damage by detergents and pesticides for which no one accepts responsibility.

The spirit of "not me" rules, and our lakes and streams have become cesspools and drainage ditches despite the best efforts of a few who have worked for fifty years to stop the pollution. Their weary cries are still heard as clashing echoes in an empty canyon.

And the skies above grow darker. Nothing is truly humorous about the cartoons we have seen depicting the future when men wear gasmasks while working outdoors. From backyard incinerators, from automobile engines, and from the gigantic industrial smokestacks come the poisons to our sinuses and lungs.

And the earth grows emptier. Who, by this time, has not heard the cries that have finally gone up concerning the depletion of our fossil fuels? But we are told not to be concerned. By proper research there will be enough left to supply the world with fuel for another hundred years! The current two or three generations will all have died off by that time and if there are any left behind, let them get along as best they can. The issue has been evident since the beginning of the Industrial Revolution. Even small children sixty years ago were asking how the world could go on recklessly pumping and digging and wasting the natural resources from the earth's depths.

Is no one guilty of wasting the earth's wealth, of putrefying the earth's atmosphere, and of poisoning the earth's waters? And is there no guilt in the uglification of the earth's surface by manmade gorges called strip mines? Is no one guilty as the earth's forests are ravaged of the last of its ancient timbers? Felling the redwoods, some of earth's oldest and tallest trees, men insist, "But it will take us more than thirty years to cut the thousands of acres that haven't been touched yet." What happens a few years from now when they are all gone? Is there no sin, no immorality in unrestrained waste of resources needed by generations of the future? Is there not true guilt in any behavior that robs or otherwise harms human beings?

Are we not aware of the lives marred every day by the abuse of children? Battered, bruised, and broken, thousands are treated each year in the emergency rooms and pediatric departments of our hospitals. The National Institute of Mental Health has reported for many years that annually more than 1.5 million children are attacked by their parents, with enough ferocity to cause injury or death. That stirs our concern, as it well ought to do.

But what of the emotional abuse? What of those children used in the making of pornographic movies in which the children are used in the expression of every conceivable homosexual and heterosexual appetite. Perverted, disturbed and angered, the odds are high that they will stagger into the world's refuse pits of degenerate souls unless by some fantastic miracle they are salvaged. But such human abuse goes on.

And it may be nearer to you than you think. Some public schools have had to remove rest room doors and children go to the rest room on the "buddy system" as a precaution against sexual assault by schoolmates of the same sex. The danger is so high and the threat so strong that some children refuse to enter the school's rest rooms no matter how strong the "call of nature."

We could go on to elaborate on other abuses to persons, such as those within the penal system, where lives are wasted in idleness. A man commits murder and is locked away into stagnant, dependent uselessness while the dead man's widow, by way of taxation, contributes to the murder's support. Why should he not be forced to productive labor with the economic returns going to the state and to support the dead man's widow and children? Or have we gone so far that such an attempt at justice would be classified as "cruel and unusual punishment?"

In the United States, we spend an average of more than $30,000 a year to confine our prisoners! During the Second World War, we housed German prisoners of war in tarpaper shacks. Those prisoners were required to work. As a boy, I talked with several who were working, under armed guard, at a local dairy in South Carolina. They were fed well and treated well, but they did not live in marble or concrete, multi-million dollar fortresses. But we are told that to declare war on criminals and house them in tarpapered wooden barracks would be "inhumane." Some people who stop acting as humans should be forced to forfeit the right to be treated as humans. But consignment to uselessness is wasteful and abusive to human beings.

We could go on to examine the extent to which mine-owners abuse their workers far beneath the earth's surface by skirting governmental regulations and failing to provide adequate ventilation and safety precautions. I've worked with patients with black lung disease. It is a destructive disease that is preventable.

Or should we examine the extent to which workers cheat their employer by failing to put in "an honest day's work for an honest day's pay." Of course, some will always counter that they are not getting an "honest day's pay."

We could examine the practices of sadistic, "knife-happy," surgeons who go on performing unneeded operations while virtually every physician who knows them "looks the other way" in a conspiracy of silence. Attending nurses shake their heads as though they have heard an unfunny joke with a punch line saying something about "self-policing within the profession." Early in the twenty-first century, we are told that North Americans annually are subjected to more than 7,500,000 (yes, seven and one half million) unnecessary surgical procedures resulting in 37,136 deaths.

Maybe those irresponsible physicians would prefer that we consider the abuses of the pulpit in which guilt is piled upon guilt as condemnations are poured out upon people already burdened with guilt and looking for relief from their heavy load.

In the event someone has missed the point, let it be said clearly: actual misdeeds are causing untold misery and harm in this world; and people, individually and collectively, are responsible for it! We are looking, then, not at guilt-feelings, but at guilt. People are truly guilty regardless of what they do or do not feel, no matter how well they have learned their lessons. Some may or may not feel guilty, but for such crimes as those just described, human beings are truly guilty.

"If it feels good, do it," in some form of paraphrase is the slogan advertisers have pasted on billboards all across our land, in keeping with the mood of the times. A politician sells his influence to redirect a defense contract. A housewife slips off in mid-afternoon to the bed of a secret lover. A builder hides the installation of inferior materials and an oil tycoon schemes to gouge the powerless consumer. But many feel no sense of guilt. Internal adjusting systems are at work.

Someone may charge that these observations are an attempt to pile a heavier load of guilt-feeling upon people. I would agree that too many are already crushed by guilt feelings. There is a proper, healthy way to deal with these feelings, as we shall see. Rather than cover it or give it a respectable name, or pretend it doesn't exist, or "psychologize" it away, a healthier alternative is available and waits offstage.

In the meantime, remember that persons who harm themselves or others are actually guilty. One is truly guilty regardless of what they do or do not feel, no matter how well he has or has not learned his lessons from experimentation or from the popular press on "How to Do EverythingYou Want Without Feeling Guilty" (cf. Vincent, book cover). Most people do not need lessons.

Absolute "Right" and "Wrong"

Some would have us to look the other way and to believe that man is never truly guilty. "There are no norms. There are no standards. There are no universal rights and wrongs. All is relative. All right or wrong is in terms of the particular culture you are observing." It is implied that we are to live in a world of pretense and ignore the collective and individual sins of humankind. And some of us tend to welcome such teachings. It helps us "get off the hook." If there is no true sin, there is no true guilt.

But foundational to modern psychology is the teaching that acceptance of reality is essential to good mental health. Can we deceive ourselves into believing that people are not being truly harmed by the kind of actions described in the preceding pages? When people are truly harmed, those who are bringing that harm are truly guilty. Again, at this point we are not discussing feeling. We are looking at actual, real, true guilt.

From all the emphasis being placed on behavior, the reader may easily, but erroneously, conclude that I am concerned only with actions. Someone may accurately declare, "You ought to be concerned with attitudes. A person's behavior is largely the outer evidence of what lies within. It is the heart that rules the head and the head that rules the hands. The seat of the problem lies in greed and envy, in lust and pride, and in the thirst for power and the hunger to avenge." That is all true, but for now let us look at that outer evidence of that which makes men truly guilty.

True guilt is in that which violates people. Psychiatrist, Karl Menninger would remind the world, "Sin is not against rules, but against people -- and it is the 'against-ness' or aggression in the intent or motivation that constitutes the designation of sin" (Menninger, p.19). And there is guilt upon those who participate in that which is against people: that which harms, demoralizes, takes away from or tears down the quality of people's lives.

But what of the feelings? The presence of those painful guilt feelings remind us of our condition – of where we are. Guilt feelings say, "You are here instead of where you ought to be. You have goofed! You have violated your own accepted standard." And if harm has been done to one's self or to another, guilt says, "You are in touch with reality." Flight from guilt feelings requires denial, fantasy, and some degree of insanity. In fact, the degree to which one is in touch with his true guilt may be the degree to which one is truly sane. Or to put it another way, the degree to which we evade our true guilt may be the degree to which we are *insane* – having broken from reality.

While I was writing the above paragraph, I was interrupted to talk with a man who had forsaken his wife and two children. He had left town with another woman who had forsaken her husband and two children. Now, months later, he is near an emotional collapse. Neither of them has divorced. He had built up an elaborate enough system to be able to carry out his initial actions, but when his defense system around his behavior began to crumble, he began to crumble. His strong sense of guilt was growing out of the fact that persons truly were being harmed. His wife was at home suffering with a broken trust in her husband. His family had been deprived of economic support and of his role as a loving husband and father. Both he and his girl friend were evading all responsibilities to their families. They both had been destroying precious qualities in themselves by their lies and their general life-style together. Since persons were harmed – others and themselves -- they are miserable in their "true guilt."

The term "true guilt" reminds us again that people often are plagued by "false guilts" in that they often feel quite guilty for violations of points in their ethical code that harm absolutely no one. Since it is obvious that we live in a world in which people are guilty, why do many feel little or no sense of guilt -- little or no sense of wrong doing?

Chapter 7

Guilty Without Feeling Guilty

Something Somewhere Hurts

Those who admit to having failed a moral obligation are likely to say that their "conscience hurts." If a counselor asks someone to put a finger where it hurts, and if the person can localize where it hurts, he or she is likely to place a finger anywhere between the top of the head to three inches below the navel. Even if they cannot point to a "place" in which they hurt, they know that something somewhere inside is hurting.

None of us likes the "guilty feeling" we experience when our inner Judge declares that we have thought, felt, or done something that violates our own inner code. As you read in an earlier chapter, each time we judge ourselves guilty, we lose some of our sense of worth, feeling worth-less: less valued in our own eyes. At the same time, we lose some of our feelings of cleanliness, feeling soiled or defiled. We also lose self-respect. Since we grieve when we lose anyone or anything that has been of value to us, each conviction of guilt initiates a fresh grief experience. In short, every time our inner judge pronounces us guilty, we lose some of our inner sense of peace. We are in disharmony with ourselves.

How do we escape that most persistent enemy of inner peace? How do we still that inner voice of accusation that demands some form of payment in some form of suffering? How do we turn off that vivid, detailed mental record of the failure to do or be as we feel we "ought?"

How do we cope with the painful inner sense of failure that tends to haunt and return, needing to be re-lived again and again? How do we live with the sense of shame that helps to make up what we call the "guilty conscience?"

The mind will take only a limited amount of pain before it tries to devise some method of relief. It needs help to endure such an insult to the ego.

We Call on "Mechanisms of Defense"

The chosen method for coping with any emotional pain is commonly referred to as a "coping device" or an "adjusting mechanism." The personality requires some means of adjusting before it can return to at least some degree of quietude. Since many feelings are experienced as an attack upon the sense of well-being, we refer to the coping methods as "mechanisms of defense." Of course, we are using commonly used psychological terms. Here, we are looking specifically at the defense against the feelings of guilt. Though we touched on the subject in an earlier chapter, in the pages ahead we will look much more closely at the many methods people use in their efforts to avoid that terrible feeling of guilt.

Many people appear to have adjusted so effectively to their feelings of guilt that they rarely admit to feeling guilty for anything. But the load of guilt is often hidden behind a veil of symptomatic behavior. One may "act out" a sense of guilt in a type of charade. Those in the mental therapy professions observe that one's pattern of behavior may serve as a clue to an underlying struggle with hidden guilt.

Keep in mind that the evidences to which we are going to look are intended to help us to recognize the symptoms -- clues to guilt. Of course, by themselves they are not conclusive evidence. Just as a headache may be a clue to anything as minor as tension headache or as severe as a brain tumor, behavior that we will discuss may point to virtually nothing at all. Or it may point to cancerous-like guilt, gnawing, eroding, deteriorating, degenerating, and debilitating, steadily destroying the whole personality. Many students of personality are convinced that of the many psychological reactions to actions, feelings, and thoughts, the feeling of guilt is potentially the most dangerous and destructive of all.

We will, therefore, look at patterns that are characteristic in our struggle to escape the pain of a guilty conscience. It should not be considered unusual that anyone would want to diminish or eliminate the pain of guilt. We have chosen means of coping with almost all pain.

If you have a tack in your shoe, you have several options. You may limp along and endure it, hoping that after a while it will go away. Or you may hope that a callous will form and grow tough enough to keep the tack from hurting, or you can "psyche' yourself into believing it doesn't exist and that it doesn't really hurt. (That can be done.) You may bend the tack over with a hammer. Or you may go buy a new pair of shoes. But you are going to do something about it even if it is only to passively endure the pain.

Pain of guilt can be far worse than a tack in the shoe. And it, too, calls for some response or combination of responses with a large number of options available. As we look at them, it may be obvious that many of the chosen options for coping with the pain of guilt somewhat overlap. However, each one may be used separately, or several may be employed at the same time. For instance, denial may be the sole mechanism as a defense against the painful feelings of guilt, or it may be used in conjunction with the use of opiates or scapegoating. At the same time, denial seems to be a part of almost all the mechanisms of adjustment to the complex feelings of guilt. Each mechanism of defense that we are approaching is different enough from the others to justify separate discussion.

The extensive material ahead is not intended to be a general study of mechanisms of defense. That is beyond the intended scope of this book. We are to consider only the mechanisms of defense used to adjust to the painful feelings of guilt! The same defense mechanisms may be drawn into service to defend oneself against loneliness, sorrow, fear, or any other potential threat to the sense of well-being. Nor am I intending to suggest that all defense mechanisms are necessarily bad (harmful). Indeed, they may sometimes help us to function and to maintain our sanity. We are only trying to better understand whatever became of guilt.

Our Inner Battlefield

The words, "strife," "conflict," "defense," and "struggle," are common words used to refer to warfare. Opposing forces, holding conflicting ideologies join alliance for strength in battle and for mutual defense. Each "side" always justifies its position and justifies the use of its particular weapons of war. In each soldier's mind, he or she is on the side of "right," and the higher the values for which one fights, the more vicious the fight and the more deadly the battle.

There is probably no field of battle with a more serious contention than those battles that go on within the human breast. We use the same vocabulary to describe the warring factions within the individual that we commonly use to refer to any other war. The words, "strife," "struggle," "conflict" and "stress" can all point to an inner struggle. Most of us know by experience the inner war between "right" and "wrong."

When "right" prevails, there is at least a temporary peace, but he errs who would speak of peace only as the lack of war. True peace exists only where harmony exists. An active war may have ceased with no semblance of peace. In most instances, only after the fighting has stopped can the opposing forces begin to work together to build a harmonious relationship. Only then will they have achieved "peace." What the world often has called peace has been only a lull between battles -- a lull used for the regrouping of forces. And the battles that have followed have been even more violent than the previous.

When "wrong" wins in the battle for the influence on behavior, there is virtually no lull at all. An even more terrible battle is in the making as new warring factions rise to contend. Those forces one has integrated within himself seem to mobilize into an underground army designed for rebellion. "Down with the ruling forces, and punish the leader," becomes the battle cry of that warring faction we call the "guilty conscience." Here is created a "no-man's-land" known by virtually every person.

Most of us have either personally witnessed the terrible ravages of war or we have at least seen the evidences of the destruction on our television screens or on the pages of our newspapers. Since the suffering and waste of human life is to be avoided in any way possible, the high command and the field commanders plan their strategy designed to reduce the enemy, but with the least cost to themselves and their own forces.

A worn adage says that the best defense is a good offense. To defend an army against the anticipated enemy attack, a surprise attack may be launched before the enemy can pull together his forces. Or the enemy's supply depot or ammunition dump may be hit in an effort to reduce his potential for battle. We may call in a preemptive strike.

Since the feelings of guilt come as an attack upon the inner sense of well-being, usually inflicting pain, we feel it necessary to defend ourselves. In the battle with the guilty conscience, we can launch a rather effective offensive defense, but the tactics are relatively few in number.

Aggressive Defenses

Repetition
Repetition is a tactic that has a callusing effect. A man who has done little physical labor during the winter may pick up his tools on the first warm day of spring and prepare the soil to plant a garden. By the end of the day, his hands may be blistered or raw. But if he works at it every day for the entire summer, his hands will become tough and callused. A guilt-producing behavior can have much the same effect. If the behavior is repeated again and again, the emotional discomfort is lost and the conscious emotional response is deadened to the callused conscience.

The callusing effect may be either intentional or unintentional. That is, one may consciously decide, "This behavior makes me feel guilty. If I repeat it again and again, I can reduce these feelings and will eventually be able to perform this kind of behavior without feeling any guilt at all. And he can do it! It is so effective that it is recommended by those who worship Satan!
(cf. LaVey, p. 53.)

But damage is still being accomplished. He is still violating the earlier formed ethical code and his guilt is hidden only from conscious awareness. The erosion of one's character goes on. The damage to the self and others goes on.

Balancing

Balancing the scales or *over* balancing the scales, otherwise known as compensation, may be thought of as a fighting attempt to save one's sense of peace. It is the exaggeration of a desirable behavior in an effort to reduce feelings of failure for not being the person one feels he "ought" to be, or for not doing as one feels he "ought" to have done. The act of compensation tends to draw attention away from the defect in behavior. It tries to "tip the scales" to make the "good" outweigh the "bad." We know that we may be far more threatened by self-condemnation than by the condemnation of others. The purpose of compensating is therefore, the aggressive attempt to preserve the endangered self.

The philandering husband may try to preserve his sense of integrity by being overly affectionate to his wife and children. "With my good behavior I can 'make up' (compensate) for the bad." "See how much I love them" distracts his attention from admitting, "See how little I love them and express it by betraying their trust in me." We must admit that some good is often accomplished in the efforts to compensate, but since one rarely feels quite "caught up," the scales always seem tipped in the direction of the bad. He has done wrong and therefore must do much more good in his effort to balance out what he has done bad. Deep inside, however, his judge keeps convicting him of fresh "crimes" that need to be balanced. Not having yet "caught up' on balancing out that for which he was already convicted, he must now try harder. Day by day the task of balancing the bad with the good becomes more and more impossible. He must, therefore, blend in additional tactics for dealing with the distressed conscience.

Confession

Confession generally is seen as a highly assertive and healthy way of dealing with our guilts. But contrary to popular thought among the religious and irreligious, confession, in and of itself is not necessarily beneficial. There is nothing automatically constructive in the act whether the confession is made to a friend, a gospel minister, a priest, a psychotherapist, or an answering machine. Philip Yancey has told of a highly popular practice in the Los Angeles region:

Guilt exposes a longing for grace. An organization in Los Angeles operates the Apology Sound-Off Line, a telephone service that gives callers an opportunity to admit their wrongs for the price of a phone call. People who no longer believe in priests now trust their sins to an answering machine. Two hundred anonymous callers contact the service each day, leaving sixty-second messages. Adultery is a common confession. Some callers confess to criminal acts: rape, child sexual abuse, and even murder (p.35).

It is not uncommon for one to decide, "I will admit my faults and will thereby purge myself of my sense of guilt." All would profit by listening to the words of Roman Catholic priest, Father Caryll Houselander:

. . . confession and self-accusation, used to escape from the suffering of the feeling of guilt, disintegrate and destroy personality. When it is habitual as with those who confess all their moral lapses to their friends, it has the effect of weakening the will more and more, until ultimately the whole character crumbles (p.53).

He reminds us also that:
The practice of continually confessing moral lapses to friends that is . . . always punctuated by exaggerated expressions of self-disgust, and go together with a complete absence of any determination to take practical

steps to break off the habits in question. Just below the surface of deliberate thought, the person indulging in these confessions reasons thus: 'I am not just an ordinary sensualist; if I were, I should suffer not like this for my peccadilloes. Only a sensitive person like myself could suffer such distress for these things.' Thus he restores his self-esteem by creating an imaginary, sensitive self who, once more, is 'not as other men,' and at the same time he is paving the way for future lapses (p.30).

Houselander has said it clearly. Confession expressed only for the purpose of relieving the pain of the guilty conscience has highly destructive potential! Why? There are several additional reasons beyond these already given.

First, open confession makes rationalization easier. "Here is what I did, but here is why I did it." Then instead of admitting reality, that which appears to be a surrender is manipulated into an intellectual mode of escape. This rationalization, blended with the cathartic "getting it off the chest" produces a bitter sweet "guilt cocktail" and a resultant temporary "high." The stage thus is set for the most destructive of guilt's force: the compulsion to self-atonement which we examined in an earlier chapter.

For confession to be healthy, it must be the initiation of a process. When confession is uncomplicated by repentance (change) or by restitution, the "high" "lets down" and one finds himself in further self-castigation. This leads to further moral lapse in the "Cycle of the Damned."

Also, confession used only as an effort to relieve guilt feelings often induces a false sense of humility, so strong that one may actually feel proud of his humility. "I'm really a great fellow to be so humble. See how great I am to admit my faults. Anyone as great as I really doesn't need to change." The positive value of confession is held for a later chapter.

In addition to the precautions already given related to confession, we must remember that confession may be only another symptom of a disease rather than an effective method of relief. Because confession induces the pain of self-humiliation, self-abasement, and renunciation, confession is sometimes used as one more implement of self-torture. Holding on to guilt for its pain and the compulsion to confess for its humiliation may be ways for us to administer the punishment our low self-image demands.

When a direct, frontal attack fails to adequately protect from the pain of guilt, we must look for some other possible ways of coping with it.

Chapter 8

Surrender To Guilt Feelings

When an army or an individual soldier can no longer fight an effective battle and is in danger of total destruction, surrender may be the only reasonable option. Self-preservation may be the only motive, but at least two additional motives may be present. Surrender may be made in order to build a true peace, but it may be only a drastic tactical maneuver. It may be made with the attitude, "I surrender for now in order to survive. You think the war is over. I am only temporarily defeated. I have lost the battle, but I may still win the war." But remember that the primary purpose for surrender is survival. Men normally give up in the face of devastation. It has happened again and again on the blood-soaked planes of Terra Firma and it has happened again and again in the guilt-soaked canyons of the mind. The spirit, in danger of being crushed in the conflict with guilt, may simply wave the white flag of surrender, "I won't try to hold my position any longer. I won't fight it any more."

That's Just the Way I Am

That's just the way I am, is a favorite form of "give-up-itis." There is no denial of the behavior that has brought harm to the self or to another, but it is a denial of responsibility. "I'm not responsible. I'm just naturally irresponsible. Poor me." When a load of guilt becomes almost unbearable, we tend to lose hope and we may throw up our hands in despair, "What's the use? I can't help it. I know I really ought not act as I dld, but that's just the way I'm made. I'm so weak, I can't resist my temptations. That's the way Papa was. It must be in my DNA."

With such an attitude it is easy to fall back on fate in any of its forms. If one is inclined toward astrology, he say, straight faced and without apology that since he was born under a certain sign that he can do no other than as he does. It is "written in the stars" that he must behave in a given way.

It is just as easy to use the fatalistic attitude and relate it to a concept of God. "I'm just the way God made me. If God hadn't wanted me to do as I do, He would have made me in such a way that I wouldn't even want to do it. What is to be will be."

Another may say, "I have to be as I am because of the way I was treated as a child." Another may add, "That's just human nature." Feelings of guilt are reduced while the guilty continue to harm themselves and/or others.

Passage of Time

The passage of time is an apparent friend of the guilty. Of course, it erases no guilt but it does have a way of dulling the pain of guilt feelings. This seems possible because of the dulling of the memory, and because one "learns to live with it" in the same manner one may learn to live with an arthritic shoulder. The pain may be always there, but after several years, he notices it less frequently; but also similar to the arthritic shoulder, it still may sometimes cost him sleep and it is there, always draining from his effectiveness.

Self-Recriminations

Self-recriminations invite pity and reassurance. Those who use it want and expect to hear, "Come now, you really aren't so bad. Look at all of your good qualities." Thus, the outside person's reassurances provide a boost to the sense of self-respect. As Karen Honey pointed out more than three quarters of a century ago, "he has such a keen moral judgment that he reproaches himself for faults which others overlook and thus ultimately they make him feel that he is really a wonderful person" (p.242). A bonus value in self-recrimination is in the diversionary benefit. He can easily cloud any issue of true weakness to his own eye or to that of another.

Everybody's Doing It

"Everybody's doing it" is a form of rationalization. Simply because the behavior is a common practice, many people experience a reduction of the sense of guilt by a form of dilution. Back in June of 1970, the Chicago Sun Times reported lie detector samplings of employees that revealed startling results. Of those tested, 72 percent of the department store employees, 86 percent of the truck drivers, and 82 percent of the bank employees had enjoyed the "fringe benefits" of theft. (Menninger, p.158) During wartime, soldiers have engaged in atrocities simply because others are doing it. When interviewed later, they have said that their behavior was no worse than the behavior of others around him.

"No worse" easily translates into "better." One thus emerges with the temporary feeling of being relatively clean. Further self-deception makes it easy to translate "relatively clean" into "clean." The defendant before the inner court then walks away with little conscious awareness of any sense of wrong-doing. However, with even the most elaborate system of rationalization, most people soon learn that a simple surrender to their impulses is intolerable to the self. Such weakness only depletes the self-image and esteem, adding to the pain. More effective means of coping with the feelings of guilt must be sought.

Chapter 9

Escape From Guilt Feelings

Those of us who flew combat aircraft with the Strategic Air Command during the days of the Korean War became intimately acquainted with the techniques of escape, evasion, and survival taught by the United States Air Force. At a special training school tucked away in the Rocky Mountains, flying personnel were taught evasive tactics for eluding the enemy and we were taught how to survive in enemy territory while working our way back toward friendly territory. We were also taught specific measures to employ in the event of capture by an enemy.

After many hours of classroom work led by highly skilled experienced instructors, flying crewmen were dropped off in mountains (similar to those in Korea) for practical maneuvers in simulated enemy territory and hunted by our instructors who took the role as "enemy." The consequences of being captured were so severe that hundreds of mothers complained to their Senators and Representatives who responded with congressional investigations. What were their conclusions? "Yes, your sons are being treated harshly. But they are being trained to come out of enemy territory alive!" Of course, not all whose aircraft was shot down came out alive, but many of those who did survive, did so because they had learned their escape, evasion, and survival tactics and had learned them well.

As we have considered already, the guilty conscience is commonly experienced as an enemy. And we sense that it can be a deadly one. The one purpose may be to stay alive. There is no simulated action, and there are no war games. We learn the survival tactics in the combat zones of life, and if we feel compelled to surrender, we know we may be tormented and left to rot in our own moral dungeons.

Those airmen mentioned in the foregoing paragraphs were taught, "If you are captured, your consuming purpose must become, 'Stay alive and escape and stay alive!'" Instructors were no "ivory towered" theorists. They were men who themselves, had escaped from prisoner of war camps. "Escape! Escape! Your purpose is to get away from your torturous captors and to get back to friendly lines." Many of those who were shot down over enemy terrain were taken captive even before their parachutes fully collapsed around them. (My Flight Engineer had been shot down over Germany during WWII. When he landed on top of a building, his parachute collapsed and he fell off the roof, landing on the steps of the building, breaking his leg. He had landed on a hospital. Hospital workers came out, took him inside, and repaired his leg. He spent the remainder of the war in a Prisoner of War compound.)

Men who fly combat missions always wonder if they will be shot down. Would they be killed? Would they be tortured? Would they die in some vermin-infested POW camp thousands of miles from home? We know the answer was "yes" for too many of them. Some were killed outright and others were tortured. Bamboo shafts were jammed beneath the fingernails. Fingers were chopped off bits at a time. Electrical shock was applied to the gonads.

We tend to cringe with only the thoughts of such torture. But the guilty conscience can torture also. As one immediately recoils from the distressful shock of an electrical impulse, one recoils from the distress of the pain inflicted by the guilty conscience. The problem continues, "How do I escape? How do I turn it off?

How do I get away from the torment? How can I keep from feeling guilty? It hurts! When a previously used method fails, we look for another. We experiment. Then we usually settle on those methods that seem to work best for us; adapting those methods that seem most effective over a span of time.

When irresponsibility and weakness of surrender is no longer tenable, bringing additional loss of self-respect, we almost instinctively turn to other patterns of thought or behavior that help escape the pain of a guilty conscience.

Suppression

By suppression of a guilt-producing experience one says, "I can't bear to look." He or she consciously tries to keep the memory of the experience out of his thoughts. The person is working to block any recall from the conscious memory. There is no clear line of demarcation between suppression and repression except that repressed material has been pushed to a level of unconsciousness. The matter is simply beyond recall. However, a person using suppression can be compared to one who is holding a tennis ball under water. Just one or two may present little problem, but try it with a dozen and you will have yourself a full-time job. Suppression is a conscious effort to forget, to push the experience and its associated feelings from the mind. In suppression one says, 'If I can keep from thinking about it, I'm all right; I'm comfortable."

But similar to the tennis balls, they keep bobbing back to the surface. By the time one is pushed under, others are popping up. The analogy may seem vaguely amusing but since guilt produces pain each time it surfaces, there is nothing funny about it. If you pictured the analogy in your mind you see a fellow quite busy at work. It can be a full-time job.

Requiring large expenditures of psychic energy, we should not be surprised that one who is working to suppress his guilt often complains, "I feel tired all the time.' Or, "I sleep all night but wake up just as tired as I was when I went to bed." Expenditures of emotional energy drain physical energy. Thus, a person with much in suppression really may be, "tired all the time." One of the most common complaints heard by physicians is related to the feeling of being chronically fatigued. The patient may go from one doctor to the next, hoping to find some physical cause for his perpetual weariness. But guilt, or the suppression of it, does not show up in test tubes or on x-ray film.

It is not only the work of suppressing guilt feelings that may leave us tired, but the act of carrying guilt adds to feelings of fatigue. Guilt is a burden that weighs heavily upon the inner person. Just as the burden of worry about the outcome of surgery faced by a loved member of the family may leave one tired, so too may the burden of guilt leave a person weary.

But it does not have to be consciously remembered to weigh heavily on us. Though lost from the conscious ability to recall at will, it may continue to be the source of inner-stress, draining the body of its energies.

Repression

By repression one actually forgets, banishing the memory of experiences beyond the ability to recall. That which is "repressed" cannot be brought to conscious thought by a simple act of the will. That memory which is too painful to be faced is "repressed" – hidden beyond normal reach in the internal "memory bank of the mind." The recollection would be too much of a threat to the sense of well-being. It is as though one faction of the fragmented self takes over a secret mission. The mission is to keep certain painful memories from the mind – those memories damaging to the concept one has of himself. As mentioned in a previous chapter, the specific painful memory may be compared to a decaying rat at the bottom of a pool. It gives off enough pollution to let a self-aware person know that something is down there that is quite unhealthy, but a faction of a fragmented self keeps moving it out of reach. Only within the most secure setting might it be permitted to rise to the surface to conscience awareness. Behind the closed doors of my counseling office, on many occasions I have watched the expressions of surprise and listened to long forgotten painful events that were suddenly permitted to rise to the surface. I suspect that most therapists feel some sense of honor to know that they have helped set the kind of accepting, secure atmosphere that has permitted the recall of old, decayed repressed memories.

Repression is an undesirable mechanism of adjustment because it is tension-producing rather than tension-reducing. True adjustment is not really made by repression. It is so thoroughly removed from the mind that one does not see the need to make any actual adjustment. The tension remains, doing its damage at the level of unawareness. Repression may be the most harmful of the many methods commonly used for adjustment to guilt.

Though it becomes a common, but unconscious, practice among adults, children can repress by conscious intent as an act of the will. In her late forties, a counselee plagued by the feeling that she was always cold, remembered for the first time, a decision to forget. "I was about six years old. It was just a few minutes after daddy had raped me. I was crying as he laid me down in the creek and washed the blood and mess off with the icy water. I remember thinking, "I must have done something that caused him to do this to me. I'm bad. I've got to forget this. I won't ever remember it again." And she did not until many years later, after many hours in the accepting, unthreatening atmosphere of my counseling office. The whole experience was repressed (forgotten). As a six-year-old child, she was not emotionally equipped to cope with the experience.

But experiences, buried by repression, have a way of decaying slowly, polluting the whole pool of life's experience. Only her feelings of the icy coldness remained as the silent signal from out of the depths, keeping her aware that some old experience with anger and guilt, was rotting away far below the surface, still taking a toll on her life. Unfortunately, and not surprisingly, her coldness was only one of the prices she paid for the privilege of repressing. Peace bought with the price of repression is always a poor bargain. When she recalled the experience as an adult, she was emotionally better equipped to deal with the memories of the event. (The counselee read and approved my telling you this part of her story.)

Knowledge

Knowledge that we are not really different, often serves as a relief of the sense of guilt. It is here that much of the benefit is gained in group therapy and in some other psychotherapeutic modes of treatment. Here also is the value in many of the popular "self-help" paperback books that line the shelves of thousands of bookstores across the land. While secret thoughts, fantasies, or desires seem peculiar and prohibitive, they have a way of inducing tremendous loads of guilt. Much of the terrible nature of many thoughts comes from the feeling that the thought or inclination is peculiar. Being "different" or holding some "unusual" trait sometimes may be perceived as a virtue, but when the trait is unintentional, it is often perceived as a vice.

Some in the field of counseling, who have repeatedly encountered those who feel guilty for thoughts or feelings that are quite common, have considered the need for a book entitled, And You Thought You Were Different or There Are Millions Like You. Or it might be entitled, The Secret Facts of Life. Despite the many college courses in psychology and the thousands of magazine articles that have been published, every counselor still sees the amazement and disbelief on a client's face upon hearing that virtually every male has had some fleeting incestuous thoughts in relation to his mother or daughter. Such thoughts are so threatening that they often are repressed. We might only wonder if even God has bothered to tabulate how many people have felt guilty for the secret impulse to defecate upon the grave of a loved one. Or we could go into lengthy discussion about those millions who feel frightened and guilty for feeling that they possess superhuman powers rivaling any god conceived by man.

The sense of guilt seems to dissipate when we become aware that we are not terribly different from others and see ourselves as "normal." But what one does with knowledge is far more important than the mere attaining of knowledge. When one is truly guilty (having truly harmed himself or others) knowledge, by itself, may lead to despair. Some in the helping professions have erroneously propagated the idea that "knowledge" is the only key to the resolution of all emotional conflict -- including guilt. But knowledge that does not lead to constructive change often leaves a person bewildered and discouraged. The endless search for knowledge may be valuable, but it is futile as long as one believes that knowledge alone will dispel every conflict in life without making any actual change.

I have sometimes had to remind clients that they might conceivably remain in therapy for ten years, learning to understand themselves in the most minute detail.

But until they took responsible steps to change their behavior, no amount of knowledge would magically change their lives or their world.

Distractions

Distraction is one of the most conscious devices people use while trying to escape by suppression. The blaring of the radio or attention to the television can be used to keep the guilty from hearing their own accusing voice of conscience. They despise the "sounds of silence," since it is during the silence that they hear the haunting voice of failure to be or to do as they feel they "ought. They strive to avoid the conflict.

Sleep

Sleep is a common requirement for the mind and the body, but when it is used excessively, we have to suspect some additional motivation. Sleep rarely is suspected as a means of fleeing guilt feelings since guilt is so commonly recognized as a robber of sleep. It does, indeed, keep many from a night of quiet rest, but for each one it keeps awake, another uses sleep as an escape from the inner condemning voice. While one person eases into the quiet, restful "sleep of the innocent," another flees to the troubled tension-filled "sleep of the guilty."

When one complains, (or others complain about him) "I don't know why, but I (or he/she) just can't seem to get enough sleep, a medical check-up should be required. An under-active thyroid gland or some other physical complication may be the problem. But if no physical deficiency is uncovered, a diseased conscience must be considered as a highly probable source of the problem.

Sexual Intercourse or Masturbation

Sexual intercourse and/or masturbation may effectively divert the mind from the attack by guilt feelings. The excitement of the experience, the memories of previous sex experiences, or the anticipation of sexual experience can all serve much the same purpose. When people are failing to maintain interpersonal relationships, it is not uncommon for the parties to feel a deep sense of guilt. The thrill of sexual arousal momentarily blocks out the feelings of guilt associated with awareness that the relationship is not as it "ought" to be.

The word "thrill" seems to be the key to understanding this mechanism. The overall sexual experience serves as the evasive action from guilt's pursuit. Within the brief moments of orgasm, the person may totally set aside guilt feelings and can simply enjoy the intense pleasure of the experience. For at least a few moments, the thrill is stronger that the sense of guilt. But when the thrill is gone, the feelings of guilt return and if the sexual experience was a violation of the inner code of standards, the load of guilt is now larger and heavier and more stressful than before.

Crime
Crime too, is often a temporary thrill mechanism. Of course, like many other methods of evading the feelings of guilt, when the deed is completed the guilt may be even stronger than before. But the thrill of plotting the crime, the enactment of the crime, and the memory of it, all serve as temporary deadeners of the feelings of guilt. And they typically leave the criminal with an economic bonus for his misdeed. His ego is temporarily strengthened. That strength is derived from having fooled the authorities. He is boosted by telling himself how smart, how cunning, or how tough he is. His satisfaction tends to nullify any sense of guilt.

Intellectual Pursuits
Intellectual pursuits serve as both escape and evasive tactics that people commonly use to avoid conscious awareness of guilt's torture. One can virtually drown

the mind in mental activity. Concentrating on an idea or theory of one's own or of another can go to such depths that one is not at all aware of the accusing conscience. We may indeed, "lose ourselves in thought," wondering in a maze of either worthwhile or worthless reasonings. The avid reader, the prolific writer or the dedicated researcher, commonly seen as an "intellectual," may be simply one who has learned an effective method of running from his inner accuser.

Forced mental activity such as the memorization of baseball batting averages and other relatively useless trivia are quite common "escapistic devices." The memorized data may be used later in an effort to gain an elevated sense of worth or status as the user impresses his peers. In addition, since an interest in athletics is commonly seen as a masculine trait in our culture, one may pump up his own sagging image of his manhood. Bear in mind that the failure to be as masculine as one feels he should be is the source of some of the worst of guilts among men. Such mental activity then may serve at least three values: distraction from the accusing voice of conscience, inflation of the image in the eyes of others, and reassurance that one is the person he or she ought to be. All three may relate directly to an underlying strata of guilt.

Work
Work, in excessive amounts, may be used quite effectively for the purpose of distraction. Evidence is seen repeatedly in the counselor's office pointing to distraction as a significant motive for workaholism. (Oates, 1971, p.5) Busy hands coordinated with a busy mind do not have time to think about personal failings.

Play
Play is commonly used in a similar fashion and is more acceptable for those having an aversion to work. It seems

more than obvious that neither work nor play are bad (destructive) in and of themselves, but it is the misuse that becomes harmful. It is that misuse that concerns us here. Then too, have we not often heard it said of someone, "He seems to *work* at playing." When play is used for escape from the turmoil of guilt rather than for refreshment and revitalization, it does, indeed, tend to become toil. Thus used, one may easily overextend himself, thus defeating the re-creative benefits of recreation. Almost any form of entertainment or leisure activity is subject to this kind of abuse.

Isolation

Isolation, sometimes called "detachment," may be considered as a form of suppression and related to repression, but is different enough to be treated separately. While "isolation" is the technical word used by some professionals, others feel that "emotional detachment" might be a better term. By cutting oneself off from the experience, the person responds as though he or she were a non-participant in that which would otherwise induce pain. Isolation is used by the self to separate, by emotional barrier, an idea or an event from its affective charge of guilt.

It is a method of coping with an experience that is expected to be unbearable. Freud saw it as a rational process drawn into protective service of the ego. When isolation is used as the defense from guilt, ". . . what remains in consciousness is nothing but an ideation content which is perfectly colorless and is judged to be unimportant." (Hensie, p.414). The event is then without affect. A prostitute has written on her experiences, "the act of sex I could go through because I hardly seemed to be taking part in it. It was merely something happening to me, while my mind drifted inconsequentially away. Indeed, it was scarcely happening to me; it was happening to something lying on a bed that had a vague connection with me, while I was calculating whether I could afford a new coat or impatiently counting sheep jumping over a gate" (Coleman, p.54).

It now seems more obvious why some therapists much prefer the term "emotional detachment" to describe this method of self-defense. Such emotional withdrawal seems rather common as a flight from what would be otherwise unbearable guilt. By use of such a denying, isolating, withdrawal, the person refuses to evaluate his or her own behavior. By "isolation," the guilty are repressing, not the event or the source of guilt, but they are repressing the value judgment that would otherwise result in the stress-producing feelings of guilt.

Masking

By masking, the guilty may hide from their humiliating self-knowledge by putting on what Caryll Houselander refers to as "psychological fancy dress.'

Psychological fancy dress . . . must not only give the wearer confidence and hide what shames him from others; he must hide it from himself. It must not only justify his conduct, he must glorify it. Guilty man is not content merely to excuse himself; he needs to boast; he craves the support and reassurance of his fellow men; he wants their flattery and applause, and he wants it exactly in proportion to his misgiving about himself. . . . the immoral woman will often see herself, not as degraded, but as uniquely pure and innocent, an emancipated human being, free of all the dirty little restrictions and inhibitions which contaminate the mind of the prude. . . She is likely to think of herself as an "enchantress" identifying herself with "one of the famous adulteresses or courtesans . . . whose sins are glorified by the vulgarity of their many envious admirers (Houselander, p.30-32).

The term "fancy dress," used by Houselander, brings to mind the fancy dress of fig leaves worn by Adam and Eve and the inadequacy of their attire that made them want to run and hide from Jehovah (Genesis 3:7). Their need for fig leaves denotes self-awareness, and self-awareness often gives one the feeling of "being seen," just as one really is. "I am revealed" can give the feeling of nudity.

Nakedness is more than physical. A person confessing often gets the feeling that he or she is removing clothing in the presence of the confessor. Therapists, aware of nonverbal communication will take note of a client who wears a coat in a warm office. The client is almost always acting out his feeling; "I have no intention of letting you see the real me today." When that client later takes off his coat, he begins to "open up" more totally unveiling himself to the therapist.

Some experimental therapists have tried to capitalize on this phenomenon of common human experience and have tried a "nude therapy" in which the patient and therapist take off all clothing at the beginning of every therapy session. In theory, if a person is undressed physically, he or she will find it easier to "undress" emotionally, thus more quickly revealing his or her inner secret conflicts. Of course, the temptation for exploitation of the patient by the therapist is more than obvious. The addition to this objection, is the fact that one physically disrobed may compensate for his physical nudity by more deeply concealing important thoughts and feelings, thus defeating the purpose, if not forcing clients to more deeply bury their troublesome conflict.

While still on the subject of "hiding, and while having been reminded of the efforts of Adam and Eve to hide themselves, we must remember that hiding is a way of trying to get out of the presence of someone. In other Biblical literature, when the Apostle Peter recognized the insight of Jesus of Nazareth, he cried out to Jesus, "Depart from me, for I am a sinful man, O Lord."

(Lk. 5:8) The guilty person wishes to stay out of the presence of the incisive and those he sees as righteous. "The incisive might see me, and the religious person further reminds me of my own failure to be as I ought." Seeing the other's righteousness often widens more fully the gap between them. The greater the gap, the greater the tendency to feel oneself as the worst of sinners, thus even further alienating from others. If I am of the chiefest of sinners, all others are cleaner or better than I. Everyone reminds me of my failures if by comparison, everyone is cleaner than I.

This hiding from others or from the self by inner deception historically has carried the title of hypocrisy. Its roots lead one back into the ideas of "covering," "hiding," or "stage play-acting." It is a deception of looking "outwardly good", but "inwardly insincere." An older root of the word suggests the wearing of a mask. Of course, like most other methods of dealing with one's destructive behavior and attitudes growing out of unresolved guilt, it is a method that prevents a solution.

Fantasy
By fantasy, possibly better known to many as daydreaming, one may direct the mind to real or fancied events that prevents from hearing the attack of the inner accuser. One's dream world seems more acceptable than the world of reality. The world of reality may be harsh, cruel and condemning. As one person said, "Because of what I keep hearing inside me, I'd like to be able to run to a world a million miles away." Then after but a momentary pause she continued, "But even there I'd still have to be with me." When the reality of the present world hurts, it should not seem peculiar that one would prefer to flee mentally to another time and another place and state of mind.

But many feel they should not daydream. Therefore, if one judge's that it is "wrong" to indulge in fantasy, the trip into fantasy then leaves them even more guilt ridden upon return to reality.

Opiates

Opiates are for deadening feelings. Therefore, when we consider that opium is among the world's most powerful drugs for deadening pain, it seems only natural that opiates rank high on any list of "escapistic" devices for attempting to deaden the pain of guilt. But since drugs often reduce the inner controlling ability, a person may perform acts while under the opiate influence that will leave him with added guilt.

Any reduction of distress is at least momentarily pleasurable, and drugs may induce their own kind of pleasurable experience. If that occurs, the person gets a psychological reinforcement that encourages him to try the experience again. As pleasurable drug experiences are repeated, he tends to become both psychologically and physiologically dependent upon that drug. It is easier to progress from there to other drugs for more satisfying reactions. Some drugs, after repeated administration, lead to the development of a tolerance, thus requiring a larger dose to get the same effect. The user may eventually need more than one hundred times the original amount to get the original type reaction. As the doses increase in size and number, the system may develop a physiological dependency. The body develops the need for the drug for its normal functioning. While one has become deadened to the feelings of guilt, he has become even more guilty of damaging himself.

Beverage alcohol, also an addicting substance, has become far more socially acceptable as an opiate escape. Possibly more subtle in its addictive powers, and more socially acceptable, it is by far the most common opiate in current use in the United States. Under the guise of having fun, one can null the painful feelings of having failed in some area of life, or even those terrible feelings of having failed in all of life.

One may try to drown the feelings of guilt, but when sober again the previous drink may only serve as fuel added to the fire of guilt. The desire to escape may be even stronger, thus adding compulsion to return to drink. Whatever else may be involved in the alcoholic's plight, the struggle with guilt is almost always a part of motive.

Self-Mutilation

Those of us who work with the severely guilt-ridden are not surprised when we learn of those who have intentionally inflicted pain on themselves as a way of punishing themselves. Observers have noted the phenomenon for thousands of years. Sophocles (496-406 BC), in a play, wrote of Oedipus who unwittingly killed his father and marries his mother. Oedipus blinds himself by sticking her golden brooches through his eyes while crying, "Wicked, wicked eyes! . . . . Go dark, for all time blind for what you should have never seen."

However, for many, physical pain is more tolerable than emotional pain. To distract themselves from the guilt's emotional pain, they cut themselves with knives or the sharp edges of broken glass. No part of the body has been exempt from injury by those who wish to distract themselves from the pain of a guilty conscience.

Insanity

Insanity is usually among the last resorts to which one may turn to escape the haunting conscience. Though normally an unconscious choice, the desperate may conclude, "I feel that I have only two choices left. I can either go crazy or I can kill myself."

At this point, the concern is not with the level of consciousness or unconsciousness that the choice is made. The simple fact stands that insanity (a psychotic break with reality) is often an adjusting mechanism used to escape the pain of guilt. One expression of insanity, the flight to grandeur, may not be so much a claim of greatness as it is a delusion of goodness. I remember a patient who claimed to be the "Father of God Almighty." Few saw the significance of his passing statement, "I am the good one." Most therapists wanted to evaluate his need for power. In one's reaction against seeing himself so terribly "bad," he may see himself as Jesus Christ or God (or the Father of God) – not necessarily as "all great" or "all powerful" but as "all good."

But insanity itself may be another source of guilt. Upon regaining contact with reality, he may recollect enough of his former behavior to feel ashamed and guilty. "I ought to have behaved differently." Any peculiar behavior of the seriously mentally ill may have this effect. "I ought to have been able to make a more healthy adjustment."
No matter what the degree of success one has in escaping the pursuing accuser, the accuser follows close behind with implements of torture in hand.

Chapter 10

Evasion of Guilt Feelings

Nobody envies a man on the run. Instead, we are likely to pity him. We tend to closely identify ourselves with the one who is hounded. In our minds we see him watching over his shoulder, or cowing in a dark corner or maybe in a muddy ditch. His sleep is listless. He is wide-eyed at the slightest noise. If he finds a haven, his stomach knots at every knock on the door. When he returns to pick up his cup of coffee, his palms are sweaty and his hands tremble. He hastily decides to move on since he fears he may have been recognized. The next person at his door may be the police.

Or we picture a lone airman shot down behind enemy lines. He grubs for roots and snails. He hears the bark of a family pet in the distance and thinks that a bloodhound has picked up his trail. He quickens his pace and wonders if he would even hear the crack of the rifle if a bullet found its mark. He hears a series of thundering booms and stops short in his tracks. It is only the pounding of his heart drumming in his ears. He spies a lone civilian and wonders if he may be a part of the small underground resistance force. He'll not take the chance. It is late in the day. He'll hide under a thick bush like a napping dog until darkness when he can move on. He dreams that he is a child again snuggling close to his mother when he is pulled from her arms by a pack of wild dogs that rip his flesh. He awakens with a start, trembling and crying like a small child. His heart pounds even harder when he wonders if his pursuers may have heard him. A sound! Who's there? It's only a fox returning to her den. Daybreak! How could he have slept all night? He's hungry. He should have used darkness for travel. He's confused. Which way should he go? He's disoriented! Is he about to run straight back into the hands of the enemy? Would he have the ability to withstand torturous interrogation? Should he let himself be taken alive? Should he kill himself and get it over with?

Ordinary men and women who work five days a week, struggling to meet the mortgage payments and fret over the crab grass in the front lawn, may be as much on the run as the men we have just described. He may be trying to elude the pursuing sense of guilt. His course is somewhat open. He can choose from a number of routes in his evasive efforts.

Sublimation

Sublimation is an alternate gratification, and one of the few positive ways of evading the awful feeling of guilt. In order to understand the practice of sublimation, it is necessary first to understand that one may feel just as guilty for impulses as for things actually done. Sublimation is as true an evasive practice as one would see. In sublimation one modifies the fulfillment of a forbidden urge in such a way as to make it acceptable. He discharges the urge by substitute activity. For instance, the man who is inclined to build a clandestine relationship with a woman of his acquaintance, instead, goes home and works to built a better relationship with his wife.

Some would suggest that sublimation should not be included as a defense mechanism since it is a way of avoiding a guilt-producing activity. It reminds us that one can know fully before the fact that he will feel guilty if he participates in a forbidden act. Sublimation, therefore, anticipates the fact and provides gratification in an acceptable, and often constructive behavior. It motivates us to more constructive action. It is not surprising, therefore, that sublimation is recognized as the defense mechanism in which there is no damage to the personality. It is one of the most constructive, complete, and successful of the defense mechanisms for dealing with guilt.

Overreaction

Overreaction goes by the technical name of 'reaction formation." It is an additional means of evading guilt in anticipation of an act. It is a response to a forbidden impulse. It is the countering of the impulse with the opposite; a means of keeping oneself from putting his own conscious or unconscious desires into action.

A child asked why a certain man had given his entire life in a personal crusade against the consumption of alcoholic beverage. Someone responded that it was quite possible that the crusader had a strong impulse to abuse the use of alcoholic beverage and this was his way of defending himself against it. Correct or incorrect about that particular person, it does show a common awareness to the use of this form of defense. "He who doth protest too strongly" is often suspect of using this defense, whether against the use of alcoholic beverage, against homosexuality, obscene literature, or some other impulse that would produce intense guilt if the desire were admitted even to the self.

Unfortunately, one engaging in a reaction formation often assumes a repulsive, self-righteous stance. His pharisaic attitude is often thinly veiled and recognized by the observer. The constant preoccupation with the moralism reveals the unconscious eagerness.

For this reason the social "do-gooder" is often resented. He is suspected of being, not so genuinely concerned with the welfare of others, as he is with his own welfare and his own defenses against hidden, forbidden impulses. If the layperson's observation concerning the anti-alcoholic beverage crusader mentioned above was correct, his crusade would not have been genuinely for the best interests of the public, but for the preservation of his own self-image.

Lest one get the idea that only the public crusader for morality may use this form of defense, it must be quickly observed that many use the mechanism self-destructively. For instance, the "Don Juanian," "womanizing" type behavior may be used by one fleeing his highly guilt-producing homosexual impulses.

Denial of Standards

Denial of the existence of true standards is highly popular among the more educationally sophisticated as a method of guilt evasion. A common argument says, "All right and wrong is purely dependent upon the particular culture in question. Rules for conduct are totally relative. It is easy then to compare some petty teachings of one culture over against those of another. One speaker may then add that none should ever feel guilty since all standards are relative. And he or she then may ask why anyone would live up to a standard just for the sake of the standard. On the surface, the position sounds quite reasonable.

But more than the wording of a standard is at stake! People are being truly harmed. Are we to believe that only a cultural influence says that a nine-year-old girl should not be raped? Is it a regional cultural taboo that forces us to cry out in rage when a five year old boy is tied to a tree, burned repeatedly with cigarettes and then strangled? Are we to believe that it is an isolated cultural influence that says a soldier must not abandon his brothers in combat? No culture admires such a person. Nor do we find a society that fails to admire the person who defends a comrade in danger. Some behaviors are universally admired and some behaviors are universally condemned.

Willie Lomanism

Willie Loman was a pathetic character in Arthur Miller's classic, *Death of a Salesman*. Refusal to form a code, sometimes called "Willie Lomanism" or "fixation," is a way of remaining a perpetual child. In childhood, expectations come from others: parents, siblings, friends and the general culture in which the person is developing.

The only person who might possibly exist without standards would be the feral child, having been reared by wild animals and continuing to live among them. Some would assume that such a person would have had no expectation placed on him by others. He would therefore feel no sense of guilt.

Then we must raise at least two questions. First, is it not possible that the animals themselves might communicate to the growing child their expectations of him? It seems somewhat doubtful that he would be able to live up to them entirely. But is it not possible, or is it not even probable, that he would expect to be able to run as fast, climb as swiftly or burrow as deeply as his companions? If he expected himself to do so, but was not able, he would be failing in his own expectations and we know that a "sense of failure" equals the "sense of guilt."

Study of written material on the subject clearly shows that most students of human behavior insist that the normal process of becoming more human requires the building of one's own inner code of expectation. This is part of the process of becoming a person. Without such an internalized code, one is something less than a complete personality. The mature personality says, in essence, "Regardless of what others say or think, here I stand; this is what I expect of me." But some refuse this significant step. Geaney wrote:

There are some people who never go through their adolescence and who spend their lives conforming to the wishes of others. Willie Loman, who lived his life to please others, was morally a child. He never operated from a core or center of gravity within himself. He was pathetic because he did not assume responsibility for life. What others thought and expected of him became his golden rule. (Geaney, 1973, p.63)

By fixating, one seems to reason, "If I don't form rules to live by, I don't violate them. Therefore, I won't feel guilty." But shuffling through life in his codeless immaturity, he will invariably injure himself and others around him again and again and again, thereby making him truly guilty.

Regression

Regression is most simply defined as "growth in reverse." In the face of excessive guilt, a person may quickly "grow backward" to a period of less conflict with inner expectations. His feelings of inadequacy and helplessness, in the face of his guilt-producing failures, urge him back to a period when he had fewer expectations of himself. If he is less mature, he nor those around him expect as much of him.

The major difference between regression and fixation mentioned earlier is that in fixation, one ceases to mature at a period of development. In regression, one has gone on toward more mature development, but returns at a later time to an earlier level of immaturity.

Some in the "talk-therapy" professions have observed that any heterosexual overt relationship, in some persons, is highly guilt-producing. The person of the opposite sex is too "holy" or too "pure" to be tainted by the sexual relationship. When the heterosexual relationship is too guilt-provoking, one regresses. Trying to better understand homosexuality, George Kisker wrote, "Since strong attachments to members of the same sex is characteristic of the early phase of adolescence, an individual may find later in life that it is easier to adjust emotionally to this earlier level than to the level of mature sexuality where heterosexual relations are expected" (p.154).

But since homosexuality is a source of guilt for many, it seems more evident that many mechanisms of adjustment to guilt are choices that involve what seems to the person to be the lesser of two or more evils. The mechanisms often do not avoid the sense of guilt, but the mechanisms used, at least reduce the sense of guilt. The attitude seems to be, "less is better than a lot." The major problem with this attitude, however, is that the guilt is simply spread out into several sources instead of centered on one source. Though more "evenly distributed," it is still there and the mechanism chosen may eventually compound the original painful sense of guilt!

Denial

Denial, in some form, probably is one of the most common means of evading the feelings of guilt. Virtually all of this chapter and, indeed, much of the entire book could be legitimately classified as some form of denial. One may gossip, lie, cheat or treat his fellow human in any number of harmful ways, but he sees himself as "good" or "nice" in comparison to others around him who are so "terrible." Some people simply will not admit the existence of evil in themselves. They will not, and perhaps cannot, allow the dark of their nature to invade their consciousness. They refuse to know it. They have formed a superhuman ideal of themselves and will not countenance the possibility of frailty and sensuality within them even as a potentiality. Denying any wrongdoing or anything negative in their attitudes, there is nothing to change nor any reason for change. There is no reason to improve. Denial of personal guilt probably is the greatest single influence that prevents modern man from finding God and rebuilding his character.

The practice of denial can be carried to almost any degree of human struggle. Carol Murphy has written of an extreme case incorporating repression into denial:

. . . a woman, committed to a mental hospital, tried to kill herself and her children. Her children died, but she survived, with total amnesia for the tragedy. She had rejected the fact of what she had done, and had, therefore, rejected the sense of guilt. But it was her guilt that made the memory of her deed unbearable. (Murphy, 1962, pp.81-84)

Police are well experienced with those who try to use denial to evade any sense of guilt for their behavior. A man may plant a bomb in a public building where scores of lives may be endangered. Before the bomb is scheduled to explode, he may try to relieve his sense of guilt by calling a warning. His reasoning follows the course: "They know of the danger. They should get out of the building. If anyone is harmed, it is really the fault of those who were injured." The perpetrator, therefore, denies accepting any sense of moral responsibility for those injured.

Even if we are not denying reality, others are ready to assist us in doing so. Several years ago, civic leaders in Akron, Ohio, considered an ordinance that would require abortion clinics to show photographs of a fetus at approximately the age of the one about to be aborted. Some reports alleged that many objecting to the ordinance were against the use of the words "unborn child" and objected to the viewing of the photographs because they would stir guilt in the woman if she proceeded with the abortion.

Many of those advocating more liberal use of abortion have insisted that women usually come through the experience, "guilt free." They show personality surveys to "prove" their point. This should not surprise anyone. The woman is likely to have gathered virtually every defense mechanism at her disposal to protect herself against feeling guilty. As long as the highly fortified defense system stands, she will not feel the sense of guilt. But since defenses often crumble, sometimes fifteen to twenty-five years after an experience of this magnitude, many in the therapy practices have seen an avalanche of guilt-ridden clients. Denial, nor any other defense will necessarily serve for a lifetime.

Ignorance

Ignorance serves as a haven amid a storm. "I didn't know the gun was loaded," ran the lines of a silly song of the 1940's. But a friend lay injured. The logic goes, "Since I did not know, I am not responsible." Lack of awareness that a behavior would bring harm to another tends to relieve guilt since intent was lacking. "I thought you had walked away," a parent may tell his child after having slammed a door on the child's finger. "I didn't do it intentionally. When no design to harm exists, one may feel relieved, unless he asks himself, "But were you not responsible to learn if the gun was loaded before you pulled the trigger," or "ought you not to have kept an eye on your child?" The feeling of failure to have acted more responsibly thus compounds the sense of guilt.

Perfectionism

Perfectionism has been called the vain "search for

glory." It says, "Forget about the disgraceful creature you really are; this is how you should be; and the wish to be this idealized self is all that matters. Oddly enough, the person using this tactic does not aim at real change in his behavior. Since the judgment of others is a major source of what we usually call guilt feelings, his aim is to give the appearance of absolute perfection. But one quickly believes his own act. Such an individual's perfection for honesty, or fairness, or compassion, does not produce a true striving for honesty, or fairness, or compassion, but produces only a drive to attain absoluteness in these qualities, which is, of course, always just around the corner or is attained in the imagination. They are not true moral standards to be achieved. They are only empty ideals.

Rigid Rightness

"I'm always right" covers the danger of feeling all together wrong. It is an impenetrable defense. It protects from criticism from within as well as from without. The person who is always right or perfect leaves no possible hole through which criticism can penetrate. No reason or logic will get through. The most glaring wrong will be neither seen nor heard. The most irrational logic will be used to justify and defend the most blatant injustice. The attitude often goes so far as to make it necessary to be right in the most insignificant and trifling details -- to be always right about the weather, or the outcome of last weeks' basketball game.

Defensive Aggression

Defensive aggression is precisely that suggested by the name -- a label used to describe the behavior of one aggressively defending himself. When he is reminded of his guilt, he turns on anger and attacks the person who reminds him of his failure. The anger felt for himself, he directs toward another. He can accept anger easier than he can accept the pain of guilt. The anger hides the feelings of guilt, not only covering as a smoke screen, but momentarily nullifying them.

This kind of reaction to guilt may be seen in the day to day interchanges within a family. The husband who feels aggressive toward his wife, annoyed and provoked by trivialities could appropriately ask himself, "What have I done wrong toward her?" Honesty with himself will usually provide an answer. A conceited parent may sit down with his child to discuss an act of misbehavior only to be countered by the child's aggressive outburst. He is not only defending himself against the parent, he is defending himself against himself. Reminded of his guilt, he has become defensively aggressive against the assault against his self-esteem.

Hate the Harmed

To hate the person one has harmed may seem at first to be a reversal of words. Few would question the fact that we have a tendency to harm those we hate, but it is not so generally recognized that we may just as likely hate those we have harmed. George Clark, a retired editor of Church Administration Magazine, was the first to call this to my attention. But it was Abraham Ross of the University of Minnesota who keenly observed this phenomenon of human behavior in clinically controlled settings. His studies conclude that with "no means of restitution available to a person, he will derogate the harmed person as a means of reducing his (sense of) guilt" (p.217). He must find fault in the person he has harmed or he must create fault (in his own mind) to make the harmed person into such a terrible creature that he truly deserves to be harmed. He tells himself, "Anyone would be justified in harming such a despicable person."

Marriage counselors do not have far to look to see this dynamic in action in those who seek their services. A husband who has deeply wounded his wife may immediately begin to find fault, or create fault in his own mind, concluding that his wife is truly worthy of contempt and the injury he has caused her. He feels justified in having inflicted the wound.

Scapegoating

Scapegoating, often called "projection," is used when one person assigns his own guilt to another. It is the projecting of the evil in oneself on to some other person. "See the look in his eye. Look at his face. Obviously, he's evil." Using projection in one's system of defense makes it quite easy to hate a person he does not even know. Using it, one can reject another or even harm another (who is projected as "deserving it") and come away feeling pure. Houselander has observed:

There is hardly an evil force more terrible than projected self -hatred. It is not for nothing we are told to love our neighbors as ourselves. We must tremble lest refusing to come to terms with all that is self, we hate our neighbor as ourself . . . . A classic story is told of Adolph Hitler who, when visiting a village where one of the cruelest purges had been carried out, wept bitterly, saying, 'How wicked these people must be, to have made me do this! (Houselander, p.8)

When one assigns his own guilt to another, there is no end to the cruelty he may inflict that would otherwise be directed toward the self.

Blame the Mirror

Blame the mirror is possibly the truest form of projection. The form of behavior is comparable to a man attacking a mirror, but in this case the mirror is another person. One sees reflected in the other, the faults he cannot bear to admit seeing in himself. He attacks the other person who has his own, or similar faults. Jesus of Nazareth spoke clearly to the practice:

And why do you look at the speck in your brother's eye, but do not notice the log that is in your own eye? Or how can you say to your brother, "Let me take the speck out of your eye, and behold, the log is in your own eye? Thou hypocrite. First take the log out of your own eye; and then you will see clearly enough to take the speck out of your brother's eye" (Matthew 7:3-5 NASB).

The anger a man feels for himself, he commonly directs toward another. He again becomes aggressive in his defense of himself. The attacker's blindness to his own faults make him quite "pharisaical," hypocritical, or self-righteous. If the one reproached sees the irony, he might respond, "Your attack on me is like the pot calling the kettle black."

There is unhealthy comfort in seeing another as lower than one's self. "I'm cleaner or better than that person." "Cleaner" is momentarily experienced as "clean." "Better" is momentarily experienced as "good." Thus, the embezzler looks down on the confidence man who looks down on the burglar who looks down on the call-girl who looks down on the street walker who looks down on the pimp who looks down on the child-molester, etc., etc., etc. Looking at the one they consider beneath them, they each momentarily experience the feeling of being "clean" and "good."

Pass the Buck

Pass the buck, another form of scapegoating says, "Don't blame me. Somebody else made me do it." I'm a victim. Here one tries to deny responsibility for his own actions with efforts to place the responsibility on someone else. It is the more conscious form of scapegoating in which one admits the behavior, but he was forced by circumstances or by someone else. After having harmed someone, he may with the speed of lightening, switch to feeling abused. . .

His terror of wrongdoing simply compels him to feel himself the victim, even when in actual fact he has been the one who failed others or who, through his implicit demands, has imposed on them. Because feeling victimized thus becomes a protection against his self-hate, it is a strategical position to be defended vigorously (Horney, 1937, p.231).

Dr. Horney, many years earlier had said that she believed the practice of blaming others for one's own faults was the "most effective" of all efforts to negative self-judgment with the resultant feelings of guilt (1937, p.246).

During the early part of the 1970's the comedian, Flip Wilson, repeatedly brought humor to millions with his properly timed line, "The Devil made me do that!" The humor seems to have come from the commonly recognized absurdity revealed in the remark so often used among North Americans. It seems to touch the nonsensical denial of reality common to many people.

Human beings want to blame everyone but themselves for their faults. A young woman, struggling with her guilty conscience for a sexual indiscretion commented, "He led me on. And he said that I could prove my love for him only by letting him do it. It wasn't really my fault." A boy in trouble with the police responded, "The fellows really made me do it. They said that I was 'chicken' if I didn't steal the hubcaps off that car."

Some schools of deterministic psychology have added to the problem. They have thoroughly removed blame from the person who actually performed a misdeed and laid it upon parents, grandparents, neighbors, and communities. The whole society was blamed when a 180 pound boy beat and robbed a 90 pound, 85 year old widow in a parking lot. When a young thug raped a sixteen year old girl, the judge blamed the permissive society and released the rapist. Reason and common sense seem to have gone out the window when such culprits are said to be only the product of the society, and that it is the society that needs changing and not the person who performed the attack. Such illogic pandered by the renowned pseudo-intellectuals temporarily salve the consciences of the truly guilty and make it easier for then to return to their loathful deeds, saying, "I'm not to blame. Even the people who are supposed to know say it's the society that makes me do these things."

As I mentioned earlier, an historic example of this "I'm not to blame" pattern of thinking occurred in Adolf Hitler. Historians long ago noted that he blamed the Jews for forcing World War II upon the Germans. In a letter he wrote just before he died, he stated:

It is true that neither I, nor anybody else in Germany, wanted war in 1939. It was wanted and provoked exclusively by those international politicians who either came of Jewish stock or worked for Jewish interests. After all my efforts of disarmament posterity cannot place the responsibility for this war on me (Coleman, p.221).

His followers seem to have generally adopted the same line of thought. Having herded millions of Jews into the gas chambers, during the War Crimes Trials, almost all blamed the officers above them whom they had obeyed without question.

When the Devil or society or superiors or peers have not been blamed in efforts to displace responsibility,

God has been blamed (Justice, 2004). A man downed a fifth of whisky, raced his car down the street, onto the sidewalk and killed two kindergarten children. Even the people of local churches tried to lift the responsibility for the irresponsible-acting driver. "I don't understand it but the Lord doesn't make mistakes." Somebody else responded, "I don't understand it either. The lord must have been trying to teach their parents something."
Almost no one spoke of the responsibility of the drunken driver!

A man watches the tires wear slick on his car. One blows out causing an accident that kills a member of his family. He calls it "an act of God," or he shifts responsibility to God saying that his loved one's "days were numbered." For those things for which men want to displace responsibility, they freely blame God or the Devil to help escape the pangs of guilt. A student brought to me the following lines attributed to Anna Russell:

At three, I had the feeling of ambivalence toward my brothers, And so it follows naturally I poison all my lovers. But I am happy; I've learned the lesson this has taught: that everything I do that's wrong is someone else's fault.

It is interesting that the concept of scapegoating has almost totally reversed in its meaning since its origin in ancient Hebrew religion. The guilty Hebrew was admitting (confessing) his moral failure and thus had a disposal problem. God had forgiven him, but he needed a psychological symbol of that forgiveness. Man needs ceremony and he needs symbols. The goat symbolically carried away his sin. It was symbolically laid upon the goat which was left to wander into the open wilderness.

Modern men often skip the confession and move directly to "laying the blame" on anything or anyone within reach. No person or group has a "corner" on the practice. While the acknowledged thief lays the blame for his theft on the social conditions, moral people of the church may lay the blame upon the pastor for the church's failure to reach its budget.

Substitution

When substitution is used as a mechanism of adjustment to guilt, people often substitute things for relationships. A woman, lamenting the relationship with her husband wept, "I have a safety deposit box full of diamonds, a Mercedes and a Cadillac in the garage and more furs and dresses than I can ever wear. My husband has never been able to understand that instead of all those things, I just want him." While he may be making an atoning payment for his guilt in this relationship, it seems that he is using things as a substitute for affection and time. He does not give things instead of love. The things he gives are his inadequate expression of love. She receives the substitute without which he would feel guilty.

Undoing

Undoing sounds illogical – and it is. But we are not discussing logic. We are discussing the things people do to escape the emotional pain of guilt. It is not at all unusual for one to participate in an "undoing" effort.

Undoing has been called "negative magic." It is so named because the person practicing this style of thought believes he can magically abolish behavior already performed. The term is not at all uncommon in psychoanalytic literature and is usually associated with some form of ritual. Ritual sacrifice, atonement, and baptism are often believed to magically undo a sinfully broken relationship, or undo the prescribed sin which has been performed. One adopting the "undoing" mechanism of adjustment is using a thought pattern similar to my patient who said, "If I refuse to believe I have

had a heart attack, I will not have had a heart attack."
This was said in the face of full medical evidence that
the heart muscle had most certainly been damaged. It
is as though one is saying at some level within himself,
"If I go through a certain thought process, or through
a certain ritual often enough, or suffer enough, not
only can I make it as though it never happened, I can
eventually erase my misdeed from history. It will never
have been." Rationality and reality do not necessarily
go together.

Displacement

Displacement is a term commonly reserved for use in
discussion of aggression, but displacement is often
used successfully in reduction of guilt feelings. A
person may reduce the feelings of guilt for some major
misdeed by displacing guilt disproportionately toward
some minor omission or deed. For instance, one may
have embezzled funds from his place of employment,
but may feel extremely guilty for forgetting to pay the
paperboy. He uses the process of displacement to "tone
down" the sense of guilt. Using displacement one says,
in effect, "O.K. I'm guilty. But not for much." He pushes
the greater guilt out of sight, while admitting the lesser
source of guilt.

Rationalization

Rationalization attributes one's actions to creditable
motives without analyzing the true and often unconscious motives. It selects an explanation that will preserve the self-esteem that otherwise would be lost by
awareness of guilt.

"I had to do it or I would have lost face."
"He had it coming to him."
"He did it first."
"Everybody else does such things anyway."

We might further refer to rationalization as the "excuses" one offers to himself or to another to explain his behavior and why he "really is not guilty" of misconduct. It is, of course, another form of dishonesty – another form of denial of reality – another form of self-deception. But even the unconscious mind cannot fully tolerate rationalization. We may convince ourselves at the intellectual level but not at the emotional and spiritual level. The inner self knows better. The inner self knows the truth.

Justification

One participating in justification seeks to prove that his or her behavior is just, right, or reasonable. He or she must show a sufficiently legal reason for a behavior. Justification is sometimes referred to as a form of rationalization. A person rationalizes to justify himself. He is trying to stay in good standing with himself or another. It has often been said that one rarely does anything he considers "wrong" until he first justifies it in his own mind – creating for oneself a good reason rather than real reason for what he does.

A salesman who has really failed to explore a newly opened market may try to justify his sales decline by finding and magnifying a fault in his good product. A man may even kill by justifying himself, either before or after the fact. "Because of the given circumstances, I can do that which I might not otherwise do." "Of course, I killed him. It was justifiable homicide." Juries rarely agree. In anticipation of an act, one may say to himself, "I should not behave as I am tempted to do. However, because of A, I am justified by doing B.

In years gone by, the hospital in which I served as chaplain placed pillow speakers at each bed. The patient could put the small disk under the pillow and listen to music or the television without disturbing another patient in the room. The speakers began disappearing almost immediately. When a nurse walked in as a discharged patient was putting a pillow speaker in his suitcase, he remarked, "Since I am paying so much for my room, I figured I had already paid for the speaker." Even in his own mind, he could justify theft of the speaker by telling himself that the room rate was too high.

But who can fully justify his own behavior? One's own efforts to do so are always incomplete. No one knows his own motivating inner forces well enough to fully justify himself. The person mentioned above who had killed and offered his justification in his own behalf was not aware that he had deeper feelings of hatred for persons in authority. A still later analysis of the killer revealed that he had a subconscious homosexual attraction for the man he killed. But he was too threatened by such feelings to face them at the time. The man he killed may indeed have been a scoundrel, but his true motivation for killing was to eliminate an authority figure and the source of his hidden homosexual conflict.

Christian theologians make frequent reference to justification. It is held that no man can fully justify himself and that if justification is to be accomplished, it will have to be done by the all-knowing, but loving God of Heaven and earth. It follows then that when one rationalizes to justify himself, his rationalization is an inadequate if not a perversion of true justification. Christian theologians see self-justification directly opposed to confession. The basic meaning of the word, "confess" is "to agree with," so that when one confesses to God, he is agreeing with God by saying, "You are correct. I have done 'wrong' when I harmed myself or another." When confession is made as an act of faith, a condition is fulfilled in preparation for forgiveness and reconciliation. Since we cannot know ourselves well enough to fully justify ourselves, Christianity encourages us to trust God to do for us that which we cannot adequately do for ourselves.

Only an all-knowing and loving God can truly justify us, giving us a right standing before Him. Whether one does or does not adhere to the view of the Christian faith, one intimately knowledgeable of human psychology must concede that it is a rare occasion in which one may fully justify his own behavior. But most of us try.

Identification

Identification in its classic form incorporates and integrates personality traits of another into the self. The process is largely unconscious. But identification, as it relates to efforts to evade guilty responsibility, is another irrational effort to justify one's behavior. It is nearer the conscious level. One may temporarily identify himself with a person of renown or one whom he holds in high esteem and says, "If that behavior is all right for him, it is all right for me. If it is all right for the president or for the movie idol, there is no 'wrong' in it for me." It seems as though one were hiding under the identification of the more prominent personality.

An additional dimension of the use of identification is more closely related to the more classical psychological definitions of identification. It requires the exercise of a lot of mental and emotional gymnastics. Here, an individual incorporates within himself a mental picture of some other person. He then thinks, feels, and acts, as he believes that person thinks, feels, and acts. This is seen in the child who has learned immoral behavior from his parents. The child who has grown up watching his parents obtain his clothing by shoplifting will have a "built in" defense against feeling guilty for duplicating their behavior as he too "naturally" steals. He may image himself, not as himself, but as his parent. He sees, not himself stealing, but his parent stealing. When he drops that identification, he feels innocent.

This phenomenon is somewhat comparable to one who puts on a mask and identifies himself as being the person whose face he wears. He steals as that person. When the mask is removed, it was the other person who stole. He walks away with no sense of guilt.

Chance

The element of chance is probably most easily illustrated by a principle applied in an execution by a firing squad. If ten men make up the firing squad, only one will likely have a "live" bullet in the rifle. The others will fire only a blank. They each choose a rifle from the rack. Each man aims directly at the heart and fires. The one man kills. But all ten members of the firing squad walk away feeling relatively innocent. "The odds were ten to one. There is little likelihood that I'm the one who killed him." If a member of the firing squad suspects that he fired the fatal shot, he can blame chance.

Chance was personified by the ancient Greeks who worshipped Tyche, the god of chance – the god that caused random unpredictable happenings. The ancient Romans called her Fortuna. You may have heard her called "Lady Luck." (She brought both good and bad.) For all practical purposes, the names Tyche, Fortuna, Luck, and Chance are interchangeable. The Romans believed this god to be the greatest of all the gods even minting a common coin bearing a feminine image. This god that personified the unpredictable and the unexpected became the most important deity of the Hellenistic era. This was because of her universal sovereignty over both mortals and immortals. Pliny, writing in the first century of the Christian era wrote of Tyche's (Fortuna's) universal rule:

Everywhere in the whole world at every hour by all men's voices Fortune alone is involved and named . . . and we are so much at the mercy of chance that Chance herself, by whom God is proved uncertain, takes the place of God (Martin, p.22.).

Dilution

Dilution by group participation is similar to the evasion of feelings of guilt by chance. This too is a means of trying to avoid guilt in anticipation of the experience. A most obvious illustration of this type of effort to avoid guilt is seen in some mob action. Murders have been committed as all members of a mob have made one stab of a knife, fired one bullet into a body, or thrown one stone. The guilt having been diluted, each member may walk away feeling, "My little part probably wasn't enough to have killed him." Everyone comes away just a little bit guilty, but no one comes away feeling highly guilty.

As Karl Menninger expressed it, "If a group of people can be made to share the responsibility for what would be a sin if an individual did it, the load of guilt rapidly lifts from the shoulders of all concerned. Others may accuse, but the guilt shared by the many evaporates for the individual" (Menninger, 1973, p.95).

Approval

Approval by an authority is the effort to gain approval of an attitude or action by someone who is viewed as a keeper of the ethic; an authority on morality. Those in religious leadership roles are sometimes approached with, "It was all right that I did as I did, wasn't it?" Or, more directly, "Tell me that what I did was all right." Such persons are really pleading, "Relieve my sense of guilt." The priest or gospel minister is seen by many as speaking directly as the voice of God, and the religious authority's approval is heard as equivalent to the approval of God.

But any significant authority may fill the need. Efforts to legalize abortion found much of its motivation coming out of the need for guilt reduction. "If we can get the law of the land to say that abortion is all right, there is nothing wrong in having an abortion," exemplifies the attitude that seeks to relieve the sense of guilt by approval of some authority.

And the Sin Goes On

We make little constructive change as long as we use any of the many avenues of escape or evasion from the truth. We continue harming persons -- others and/or ourselves. And we have noted that with few exceptions even the coping methods used to relieve guilt feelings are in and of themselves self-defeating. But they are all chosen as survival techniques. As Menninger said of men's coping devices:

Some . . . are properly classified as sins. They are aggressive, expensive, unpleasant, hurtful, even obnoxious, but they are all to some degree lifesavers for the actor! Whether sin or crime or symptom; every one of these devices represents an automatically chosen lesser evil, and an attempt to make the best bargain possible. Given the experiences of the particular individual, the set of psychological structures in his personality, the environmental situation as he perceives it, the stresses felt and the choices open to him, his strange act seemed to him "a good thing at the time" -- indeed the only right thing at the time. But most of these compromises and decisions are made without much involvement of consciousness or reason. . . . Self-preservation is everybody's motive every minute, all the time, but so is a trend toward self-destruction. These two drives are in constant operation and opposition. Because of them we are constantly and continuously trying both to self-destroy and to self-preserve, to stay alive in spite of ourselves. (Menninger, 1973, p.92)

In the early chapters of this book, we looked at the consequences of hearing our inner Judge declare us "guilty." We had sinned. We had failed to live up to our own expectations of ourselves. We had behaved in ways that had harmed ourselves and/or another. We saw the terrible consequences of trying to make ourselves pay for having violated our inner code -- own sense of morality. We recognized that we are in danger of entering the "cycle of the damned."

In an earlier chapter, we examined the various ways that our inner Defense Counsel works to keep the Judge from declaring us "Guilty." And now we have looked at ways we try to protect ourselves from being punished after having been declared "guilty." But our methods of dealing with guilt have been highly destructive. The person is truly cursed – truly damned -- who succeeds in building such a successful wall of defense that he never sees himself as guilty.

We have descriptive labels for such people. We sometimes call them "psychopathic" and sometimes "sociopathic" personalities. For all practical purposes, the terms are interchangeable. Each therapist has his or her word of preference and they usually cannot tell you why they prefer one over the other. Since I usually prefer the word "psychopath," that is the word I will use as we continue to examine guilt and its feelings or lack of associated feelings.

In brief, the psychopath has little or no detectable sense of conscience. Our prisons are packed with them. Hundreds have been tested, quizzed, and evaluated by highly trained and experienced members of the psychotherapeutic professions. Why does the psychopath feel no detectable sense of right or wrong? During some of the time that I have been writing this book, a man has been on trial and convicted of murdering his wife and child. Prominent television personalities have asked repeatedly, "How can a man kill his wife and child and seem to have no remorse?" Those who have given psychiatric evaluations keep saying, "He's a psychopath. In his own mind, he is amoral. He does not possess the normal human capacity for experiencing any sense of wrong-doing." Why? Why do some people not have the capacity to experience guilt? No one is certain. Theories abound. You have been reading part of mine.

I suspect that the psychopath is simply a person who has woven together many or most of the defenses that I have catalogued in the foregoing chapters. When I first wrote this theory roughly twenty-five years ago, in the book *Guilt, the Source and the Solution* (Justice, 1981), I thought that therapists from all over the United States might write me to debate. No one ever questioned my conclusion.

After having studied issues related to guilt for more than forty-five years, I am saddened by the awareness that I have never known, nor have I read of a psychopathic person having been saved from his or her self-destructive process. I have envisioned the psychopath as a disintegrating remnant of a human being, on a steep, snowy, icy hillside. The farther down the slope he slides, the faster he slides. Each evil deed propels him a little faster toward total destruction. He is unaware that he is becoming more and more disintegrated and is oblivious to his own pending doom. It appears that the psychopath has passed the point of no return – having gone beyond the call of redemption. He may lie, cheat, steal, maim, rape, or kill. He sees no reason to change. He sees no reason to cry out for help.

Whether one feels highly guilty and tries to make himself pay by self-punishment, or he feels no sense of guilt whatsoever, both end up destroying some of their most precious human characteristics. The wages of sin really is death.

Recall the Law of Mortigression

Recall that in an earlier chapter, we discussed the fact that in our own inner courtroom, when our angry inner Judge declares us "guilty," that Judge decides to make us "pay." And the payment must be made in the form of punishment. Consequently, WE EACH WORK TO GET FOR OURSELVES THAT WHICH WE FEEL WE DESERVE! When we feel we need to be punished, we must bring pain to ourselves. But without fail, that punishing behavior that brings us pain only makes us even guiltier; and if we are reasonably emotionally/spiritually healthy, we feel guiltier! We feel that the fresh guilt now calls for more punishment. Thus we are back once again to the "cycle of the damned." Guilt calls for punishment that produces guilt that calls for punishment that produces guilt that calls for punishment . . . .

Remember the law of momentum. When applied to the personality, we called it the "law of mortigression." Since this term is new to you, it needs to be repeated. "A personality in the process of deterioration tends to continue in the process of deterioration unless acted upon by an outside force."

Chapter 11

We May Appeal To The Highest Court

One outside force is needed to stop both the erosive behavior that produces the ongoing sense of guilt and the need to reduce the pain of the guilty conscience. That force is LOVE, and the guilty need to experience it as the grace of FORGIVENESS.

The dynamic force of love seems to be recognized by humankind in every level of civilization. Its presence, or lack of presence, is seen in almost every facet of every culture. Look at the people's art, their literature, and their legend. Look at their music and their religion. Look at the laws men have made. Love, or the lack of love, is among the must powerful forces known to the human race.

Love, experienced in forgiveness, reduces the guilty conscience to only a memory with regret. This kind of love works only for the best interests of the recipient. It holds no grudge and demands no payment. Indeed, if one tries to receive it by making a payment, he does not receive it at all. He must receive it as a gift. Go try to buy love. What you receive is only an empty, meaningless symbol of what love could be.

Every counselor has experience with those who have spent a lifetime trying to get someone to love them. They have tried to barter for love by offering good behavior, or loyalty, or labor, things of value -- even their bodies. While love may be offered, in reality, the one trying to work or earn it, experiences something less than love. I'll say that again. Genuine love may be offered. But if one is trying to earn it, it is experienced as something short of love. For love to be of value to the receiver, it must be experienced. Love will be received freely, or it will not be received at all.

God loved the world (folks like you and me) so much that He gave his only begotten Son, that whoever believes in Him – keeps on trusting Him would not perish, but have everlasting – eternal – unending life (zoe – spiritual life, as compared to bios – physical life) (cf. John 3:16).

Inadequate Payment

Instead of damning ourselves by trying to make ourselves pay for violations of our own or of God's law, God knew that no payment – no atonement that we make can ever fully satisfy even us. We always keep demanding more. Working with those who are aware that they are trying to make themselves pay for their misdeeds, I've asked, "How much more do you feel you will have to pay before the debt is fully paid?" They have seemed astonished when they pause to realize they are working toward paying ultimately with their life. One said, "I feel that I won't find peace until I see my own blood spilt out." After pausing to reflect, she continued, "But even that price wouldn't be enough!"

In a previous chapter we thought about the sacrifices offered in appeasement to an angry god – the deified self. The little deity that human beings have created has angrily required the shedding of blood in payment for wrong-doing. Biblical history records that the sacrificial shedding of the blood of a prized animal gave some temporary feelings of relief from the burden of guilt. But Jehovah God made it clear that unrepentant and rebellious people were fooling themselves if they claimed their sacrifices were for Him!

Through the prophet Isaiah, Jehovah said, "Hear the word of the Lord, you rulers of Sodom! Give ear to the teaching of our God, you people of Gomorrah! What to me is the multitude of your sacrifices? says the lord; I have had enough of burnt offerings of rams and fat of fed beasts; I do not delight in the blood of bulls, or of lambs, of he-goats" (Isa. 1:10-11).

Jehovah further spoke by way of the Psalmist. "Do I eat the flesh of bulls, or drink the blood of goats? Make thanksgiving your sacrifice to God, and pay your vows to the Most High; and call upon me in the day of trouble; I will deliver you, and you shall glorify me" (Ps. 50:13-15). The psalmist further declared that with the blood sacrifices, Jehovah required the offering to Him of a broken and contrite heart. (Ps. 51-16-17). At the same time, however, the Old Testament book of Leviticus (Chapter four) records that Jehovah had called for the practice. He was instructing them to perform acts beneficial to them, His people. The blood sacrifice was a means by which a sincerely penitent Israelite could express both; faithful obedience to Jehovah, and actually identity with the sacrifice slain and offered on the altar as a substitute for the worshipper. A blood sacrificial payment was (and is) a need of man, but no atoning sacrificial payment has ever been adequate, to God or to one's self, without a penitent heart.

Payment in Full

Knowing the human need for a payment to be made for their wrong-doing by suffering, God provided what man required! "For God so loved the world that he gave his only son that whoever believes in him should not perish (destroy himself) but have everlasting life (Jn. 3:16). God's fullest revelation of Himself, Jesus Christ, came to give Himself for man's redemption; that is, He gave Himself – ultimately His life to free man from the grip of his own destructive behavior and its consequences.

On the cross, He filled the role of the "suffering servant," as foretold by prophets many years before His birth. Of course, the prophets recognized that their people were a self-centered rebellious people. The prophets also knew that their people were attempting to punish themselves in an endless cycle of further immorality that was destroying them, and that neither the self-punishment nor the shedding of the blood of animals in further atonement was an adequate price. It was not enough for them, nor was it enough for Jehovah their God, unless it was accompanied by remorse and changed behavior.

The "suffering servant," Jesus Christ, permitted Himself to be cruelly lashed with a leather whip (similar to the "cat of nine tails") and He accepted a crown of thorns to be jammed down upon His head. He permitted nails to be driven into His hands and feet and accepted a slow, excruciating death upon a Roman cross. Jesus took suffering upon Himself so that we would not have to continue making ourselves suffer.

Jesus paid the price we demand. As described in preceding pages of this book, when we have done wrong, before we can accept relief, a price must be paid. It has been paid already! I am speaking about a vicarious atonement; an atoning payment made by one person in another's behalf. For each of us, Jesus paid the price. He was the sacrificial Lamb of God who voluntarily gave his life as a ransom (freeing price) for all (cf. 1 Tim. 2:6).

Paying for one's own misdeeds seems to us to be the right or correct way, but "There is a way that seems right to man but the end thereof are the ways of death" (Prov. 14:12). The Author of Scripture, long ago, was also aware of this need for man to try to pay for his own wrong-doing. If one sees the folly of his attempt, he has room for hope. Only when one sees the impossibility of ever satisfying his or her own inner sense of judgment, will he cry out for help. Only if one sees the potential future of his course of behavior and the destruction ahead, is he ever likely to seek assistance.

There is a way out of the hell which men create for themselves -- a way out of that hell that begins here and continues beyond the grave. But that way out requires nothing less than a miracle – a miracle that began thousands of years ago and is still happening to this day. It began in a personality, at least as early as the coming of God in Jesus of Nazareth. That coming in the flesh is commonly referred to as the "Incarnation." Jesus, whose name means, "Jehovah Saves," came as "Imanuel" (God with us). Giving Himself as an atoning payment, He made possible our salvation, our deliverance, from our own misbehavior and the ensuing "cycle of the damned," here and hereafter. His gift is available to all who will sincerely, repentantly ask for it and willingly receive it.

But asking for help requires a degree of humility from which many rebel. It brings to light the stubborn streak. "I am too strong and able, or undeserving, to ask for help from anyone – even God." Only as one sees that no amount of suffering can ever earn his release from guilt, can or will, he ever cry out, "Help! Can anyone pay it for me?" At this point another voice cries out, "Paid in full! Accept the payment that has already been made in your behalf! It was paid for you nearly two thousand years ago at the cross and I am still paying!" The concept of one paying for another's wrong may be as old as the human race. It is certainly as old as the cross, and as fresh as the daily life we now live.

No, having another pay is not what the guilty deserves, but it is at the very heart of the concept of "grace." Grace has been defined as, "the unmerited favor of

God," or it may be called an "unearned gift." The gift is FORGIVENESS! Only as we accept that unearned gift will we ever find release from "the cycle of the damned" or from the inevitable process of erosion of the personality. Only in forgiveness will the inner judge stop demanding further punishment – further atonement. Only then can the inner executioner find rest. Only in forgiveness will any guilt-ridden person find peace. Only then will the curse be lifted. Only then does one experience the peace of God that passes all understanding.

Since forgiveness cannot be earned or merited, it must be called a "grace." Any unmerited act of kindness or favor extended by one person in behalf of another is an act of grace. If it were "earned" it would simply be a swapping or bartering of benefits. I will do something nice for you if you will exchange by doing something nice for me. Such bartering is not a gift. Though we have been considering the grace of forgiveness, we could go on to speak of the grace of patience, the grace of understanding, the grace of compassion, the grace of mercy, the grace of His leadership, the grace of His encouraging presence, . . . and on and on we could speak of God's gifts to us which we have not earned. These are gifts offered to any who will accept them. Not because any have earned the right to them but because it is the nature of God to want to give. They will be received as free gifts or they will not be received at all!

Recall that the law of mortigression makes reference to "an outside force." Only an outside force can stop the down-hill process and direct the general course of the life from its destiny with final destruction.

The demand of the internal judge for "payment" seems never to change. Suffering of some kind is required before the guilty can find any sense of release from the necessity to pay. But fortunately we have, also, the capacity to accept the "payment" of another for our own wrongdoing.

Follow with me the struggle of Helen and Bob who, of course, have given permission to tell their story. They asked only for me to protect their identity.

While Bob was overseas on military assignment, Helen became lonely and turned to Bob's best friend for companionship. Caught up into the emotion of the deepening relationship, one evening, they engaged in a sexual relationship. Helen's sense of guilt became overwhelming. She became despondent, with a mixture of feelings, wanting Bob to come home and dreading to see him again. When he finally came home, nothing seemed quite right between then. Helen simply could not respond to her husband's affection and was convinced that it was because of her experience with the friend. Hoping to unburden herself, with great shame, Helen confessed to Bob that she had, during their time apart, engaged in sexual intercourse with his friend.

Bob's response was about as emotional as if she had casually mentioned that it had rained during the night. He told her that he forgave her and in no way would hold it against her. For the next four years, the relationship between them grew from bad to worse. In desperation they turned to their pastor who referred them to me for marriage counseling.

Little developed during their first counseling session. I thought it significant that neither evidenced irritation with the other. Neither expressed big complaints except, "We're just not happy together." After a few moments of the second hour in the counseling setting, Helen hesitantly commented that she knew what was wrong in their marriage. "It has something to do with my having had an affair several years ago when Bob was away." Without stopping, she told the whole story of what had happened.

As she finished the last detail, Bob broke into uncontrolled sobs. With his face in his hands, his shoulders heaved. Helen sat in open amazement. Her jaw dropped as though she could scarcely believe what she was seeing and hearing. As Bob sat up trying to control himself, her voice further revealed her astonishment. "But Bob, I didn't know I had hurt you! You seemed so unaffected years ago, when I first told you, I thought you didn't love me enough to be hurt by what I had done. I thought you didn't care enough to be hurt!" They cried together for a while. Bob explained that as soon as he was alone, he had "cried his eyes out." "I was torn to pieces but I didn't want you to know. I didn't want to hurt you more by having you see how upset – how hurt I was."

"But Bob, when you said you forgave me, but obviously weren't hurt by what I'd done, your words of forgiveness didn't mean anything to me. I've prayed for God to forgive me but nothing has given me any sense of relief of my feelings of guilt." Bob reassured her that in spite of his deep feelings of rejection, and his sorrow for what she had done to herself, he really had forgiven her and had never held the experience against her. Amid laughter and tears she heaved a sigh of relief and cried out, "Oooooooh God! At last I'm free!"

My day was brightened ten years later by their pleasant note from across many miles telling me of their deepening relationship that was still in process. That experience with them confirmed for me once again that wrong-doing demands payment and that the offender must know of the cost before forgiveness is acceptable!

In this experience, we witnessed a vicarious atonement – one person making an atoning payment in the other's behalf! It was her need! Before she could feel the sense of release from feelings of guilt, she had to know that the offended one had suffered because of his deep love for her.

God provided what we humans need. Before any person can find true and lasting release (redemption) from guilt, the one most offended had to suffer. For this purpose, in our behalf, Christ accepted and suffered death upon the cross. The curse of death that men place upon themselves can be lifted because of the curse of death laid upon Jesus Christ. Before His birth, it was revealed that the Christ was to be called Jesus (meaning "Jehovah saves"), "for he shall save his people from their sins" (their destructiveness) (Matt. 1:21).

Seeing the harm we bring upon ourselves, He was (and is still) wounded by our transgressions. Though Jesus Christ suffered the pain of the whip and brutal crucifixion upon the cross, He is still suffering because of our behavior. Our sin hurts God now and He still is paying the price for loving us.

In what way is He still suffering because of our misdeeds? The answer to this question involves the meaning of "love." Any father who loves his children hurts when he sees them hurt themselves or when they hurt one another. I remember well the tears of a father who had seen the nude photograph of his daughter in the centerfold of a popular magazine. He was heartbroken to realize the degree to which his daughter was degrading herself. Surely God's capacity for love is far greater than ours as human beings. If we are hurt by seeing those we love harming (or degrading) themselves, how much greater must be the hurt of God who loves far more? Since He loves, He is still paying a price daily for loving us.

A paradox that is further defeating sometimes exists in the very highly guilt-ridden. Though the person may feel crushed beneath the load of guilt, and despondent, nearly to the point of incapacitation, there can be pomp in acclaiming, "I feel I'm the worst and most evil person ever to live." The pomp grows out of the feeling,

"I have achieved distinction." Though negative, it is a distinction. With this claim often comes the feeling, "My sin is so great, I feel that even the shedding of the blood of Christ is not enough. I still feel I ought to have to pay.' There is hidden within this statement the attitude, "I am superior to God. His blood -- his death, is not enough, but mine would be." This attitude is often accompanied by a feeling of super-humaness that has the ability to transcend death. The victim of such guilt tends to feel that he or she somehow will be able to look back with satisfaction for having paid the supreme price. Of course, we are seeing in such a person, a very highly suicidal individual in whom the wish for death is no longer hidden far beneath the surface of the mind. "Without the shedding of blood there is no forgiveness of sin" (Heb. 9:22). This suicidal person insists that his own blood must be shed to gain release beyond any provision that God has made in Christ's death and subsequent resurrection.

It should not be construed that only the terribly immoral can become the victim of the internal judge who screams, "Pay!" It is often, as Freud observed, ". . . those people who have carried saintliness furthest who reproach themselves with the worst sinfulness . . . and it will be said that a stricter and more vigilant conscience is precisely the hallmark of a moral man" (p.73). Unless even the pious repeatedly returns to accept forgiveness from the One who has already paid the ultimate price, the pious man too may fall prey to his internal executioner. This executioner's task is to execute punishment to whatever limit permitted by the internal judge. Upon him who turns from the grace of God's forgiveness, punishment may become quite cruelly executed. It was reported by the highly reliable church historian, Eusebius that the early church father, Origen castrated himself because of the temptations he experienced while giving religious instruction to women.

A former theology student once told me of his sense of shame and guilt for having failed a course in his studies. He went on to say that after his academic failure he had quit a good-paying job because he felt he did not deserve it. Without forgiveness, the internal judge will extract payment of sinner and saint alike.

Once recognizing that God paid the price of every man's release from the grip of self-destructive behavior, one may yet be far from accepting that price in payment for his own individual wrong-doing. There can be no debate that forgiveness is for the receiving and that there is no way to earn it. But there are some requirements laid upon him who will receive forgiveness.

A foremost requirement is the willingness to receive. The requirement is somewhat similar to my son's offering to me a bite of his candy. I'm expected, at least, to open my mouth and then to bite down when he places it between my teeth.

God is not going to force His will upon any person. He is no more determined to force His gift of forgiveness upon us humans than is a child going to force us to take a bite of candy. It is up to the individual to be a willing recipient, for which some preparation is necessary. Let's look at the preparation.

Socially Acceptable Idolatry

Refined men of the modem era rarely carve idols of stone or wood. Instead, they make idols of flesh and blood. Men make idols of themselves! The man who refuses to listen to the voice of God listening instead to the voice of his own desires, is not putting himself on a par with God but is, in effect, putting himself above God. He is in the act of self-deification. "Nobody is going to tell me what to do. Your instructions may have been good for another day in another generation, but I'll live by my own desires. I know what is best for me. I'll be absolutely free." There is the arrogant pretension of being the true No. 1. With this attitude one seems to bow before the image of himself and pray, "All hail. Thou alone art worthy of obedience and trust. Your private desires and passions transcend all the laws of God and humankind. Only you are adequate to pay (atone) for my sin."

Reverence for God is the beginning of wisdom. Only when I renounce my own deified self, am I beginning to accept the deity of Jehovah, the God of Creation and Recreation. This truth is as basic as the words from the Shema of the Jew, ". . . Jehovah is our God. He is one." And it is as basic to the Jew as the earliest common confession of the Christian faith; "Jesus Christ is Lord."

Confession

It has been said that confession is somewhat comparable to opening the door to a packed junk-room. At first, only clutter on top and in front can be seen. Much lies beneath that has been forgotten. Most is old and musty. Only as stuff is removed and examined do we begin to remember what has been lying there covered up all the time. Much that we thought was lost is found to be decaying, contaminating everything it touches, and giving off the bad smell that has been seeping through the cracks, occasionally causing embarrassment. The things we remember being there are bad enough to make us feel that we would rather keep the door closed.

The dread of facing the memory and consequences for our misdeeds often leads to a denial of their reality. As stated in an earlier chapter, denial is one of the most readily available defenses that any person is likely to use. We are inclined to deny to a fellow human being, to God, and to ourselves. We will persuade ourselves to believe as long as possible that no one as good or as intelligent as we would possibly do as our accuser says. Humans are masters of deceit, even to themselves. It is nothing less than a flight from reality – a trace of insanity – but it is a common characteristic of virtually every person at some time in life. It is as though one says, "If I admit the truth about myself, I will hate me!" But the hate is there anyway, even though one refuses to admit the cause!

It is painful and frightening to admit that our behavior is harming ourselves and others and that we are headed for destruction. It is also humiliating to admit that we could be foolish enough to behave as we sometimes do. Silence helps make denial possible. I've often heard persons trying to gain the courage to analyze their own behavior, "I think I'm about to see something about myself that frightens me. I don't want to say it, because if I hear my own voice say it, I'll have to admit that it's really true." This points to one of the major benefits of the act of confession. Once one admits a truth aloud, it is much harder ever to hide from that truth again. Also in the act of confession, we grow closer to accepting responsibility for our own behavior. We, as erring human beings, would rather blame anyone else than to accept our own responsibility. We will blame the circumstances, the culture in which we live, or anything or anyone we think we can get away with blaming.

When I confess to another human being, I am admitting that I know the source of my pain. I know the source of my troubled mind. I am admitting that I know my own behavior is defeating me. The word gnosis in the New Testament Greek, means "knowledge" that is thoroughly comprehended. It can mean cognitive, sexual, and mystical union at the same time. It is an integrated truth. The word 'insight" has been given a similar meaning in our day. Paul Tillich called attention to this in his Systematic Theology.

. . . the term "insight" has been given connotations of gnosis, namely, of a knowledge which transforms and heals. Depth psychology attributes healing powers to insight, meaning not a detached knowledge of psychoanalytic theory of one's own past in the light of this theory but a repetition of one's actual experiences with all the pains and horrors of such a return. Insight in this sense is a reunion with one's past and especially with those moments which influence the present destructively. Such a cognitive union produces a transformation just as radical and as difficult as that presupposed and demanded by Socrates and Paul. For most of the Asiatic philosophies and religions the uniting, healing, and transforming power of knowledge is a matter of course (p.96).

Jesus said, "Ye shall know the truth and the truth shall make you free" (Jn. 8:32). In truth is the freedom for healing, freedom for growth, and ultimately freedom from the burden of guilt.

As I insist on the value and need for confession, I am not at all making reference to the dead, formal, mechanical confession that has so often characterized the practice. It is not at all necessary for every person to confess to another human being! Many can confess only to God and find the relief that is needed. For those who can confess only to God and gain the needed lifting of the burden of guilt, and the needed reconciliation, no further confession is necessary. But many have confessed only to God and have still found no relief. It is that person who needs another human being to hear the confession. And if another person has been injured, that injured one must be included unless doing so will cause additional harm. We will return to this subject later.

As I work with people I'm always listening for clues that will reveal whether the person basically likes or dislikes himself. True, persons seeking counsel usually are hurting somewhere in their interpersonal relationships, or they would not have come to me. One aspect of the troubled relationship is the counselee's responsibility for part of the discord, and at some level of awareness, he knows it. For this, if for no other reason, he has some self-dislike.

During my earlier years in training, I was taught that the ability for one to see one's own sense of self-dislike, the need for punishment because of that self-dislike, and the method used for punishing, were all buried deep, deep in the unconscious. Certainly much of it is far beneath the surface and is slow to emerge. However, my experience of intensive work with many hundreds of persons has convinced me that much of it is not deep at all!

After feeling I have established rapport, I have many times observed, "I get the feeling you don't like you." With few exceptions, the person has affirmed my observation and has consented to tell me why.

That person who is admitting the reason he dislikes himself is confessing. Possibly one of the greatest tragedies of the Protestant Reformation was the removal of confession from almost all of the religious groups that formed and later developed into "denominations." Some important truths of the scripture have been neglected in that omission of confession. In the original language of the New Testament, Greek, the word commonly translated "confess" means, 'to agree with." When one confesses before God, he is agreeing that his behavior has been in error. His behavior has been "wrong." It has been "incorrect.' Confession admits, "I have been 'wrong.'"

Both Jesus and Paul clearly taught that God's Spirit dwells within those who live in a trusting relationship with God. Therefore, if a person is admitting his wrong to a person in whom Christ dwells, confession to that person may be also a confession to Christ. The promise recorded in Holy Scripture stands, "If we confess our sins, He (God) is faithful and just to forgive us our sins and cleanse us from all unrighteousness" (1 Jn. 1:9).

A young woman who came by my office and asked to talk with me, spent an hour that first day in general conversation. A week later she spent another hour, talking only of surface matters. I suspected that something more important had brought her to me. We would have to build a relationship before she could gain the courage to talk about it.

The third time she came, she dropped heavily into the chair and said she knew it was time to talk about what had been on her mind since before our first conference. I sat quietly listening as she tearfully, embarrassingly, confessed degrading, self destructive acts of immorality that violated every principle of virtue she had ever been taught as a girl. She held only contempt for herself, feeling cut off from God and isolated from the world of decency. She talked a while and cried a while, and then repeated the cycle. After nearly an hour of agonizing confession, she again wiped away tears, batted her eyes several times and looked intently at me. Her voice grew calm and warm.

"Chaplain Justice, this has been the strangest experience. It has seemed as though you were pushed back and Jesus has been standing between us, listening to me. I've been talking to Him." Moisture burned my own eyes as chills literally ran up and down my spine. She had opened the door into the most "holy place." We two sat in the presence of a Third. It seemed as though within her soul she heard, "Neither do I condemn thee. Go thy way and sin no more. Thou art forgiven."

For another two years I joyfully watched increasing evidence of the re-creative, redemptive miracle of love and grace as God continued to work in her life. She later joined the Peace Corps, and the last I heard of her she was a nurse serving as a missionary in Africa. Wherever she serves Him today, I doubt that either of us is going to forget the day she came face to face with our Savior. And I had the great privilege of having been present when it happened.

It is true, few have as vivid an experience as this girl did, but it is quite common for one to leave the confession experience feeling cleansed and forgiven. While many who come confessing are far from ready to face God with their guilt, others find it helpful to bow reverently and penitently in a prayer of confession. The words are clear, "Confess your faults one to another, and pray for one another that you may be healed" (James 5:16). The word "healed" elsewhere in the New Testament, is repeatedly translated, "saved."

Dennis Geaney speaks clearly to the matter of encountering God within another human being. To get to know ourselves through confronting our past in the light of our present behavior, we need others. We need people to reflect on our present behavior and to take us by the hand as we walk through the dark and treacherous caverns of the past. We need the grasp of a firm and loving hand as we start the journey and the supporting embrace or the 'You're O.K.' of another as we look again at what frightens the child in us. We are describing here the way which one comes to terms with and erases the neurotic or pathological guilt. It does not differ from the way we achieve holiness or wholeness. (p.98)

In addition to the resistance to confession already discussed is the fear of trusting. The thought of another person knowing our faults is painful, but knowing that what we say could be repeated and made public is terrifying. Who has not had his or her confidence betrayed by someone? Once was enough! To a friend we said something we expected to be guarded and secret. Later, we learned it had been told. We felt betrayed. We hesitate to confide again. We distrust. Obviously, we must choose carefully one in whom we confide. With competent therapists in their own home-town, couples have driven more than 600 miles a week to discuss with me their marital problems. Although I have worked to maintain a good reputation, they came to me because they were afraid to trust a local marriage and family therapist.

We have at least one more reason to fear confession. It lies in the fact that the guilty feel a sense of contempt toward themselves. "I know me and therefore I disrespect and hate me. If I tell you what kind of person I am, you will hate me and lose respect for me, too." The most we who anticipate hearing confession can promise is that we will try to accept the confessant (the person confessing), despite what we may hear. We may silently hope and pray that we will have that capacity to continue to respect them after hearing their confession. Verbal assurance that God still loves them often seems meaningless. It will usually become meaningful only as the confessant finds love and acceptance in the relationship with the confessor.

Since confession is painful, many people conclude, "I want a quick solution to my guilt problem. I'll try a short-cut to relief." They may not express themselves in those exact words, but in attitude and effort they are saying just that. "Quickie" solutions are among the greatest problems facing the person wanting relief from the burden of guilt. We may have spent long years filling our "bag" with guilt and its shame. Many then take a walk down the aisle of a church, offer a two minute prayer, attend a few hours of instruction mixed thoroughly with the waters of baptism and expect instant total salvation. Maybe some few attain it, but many come away confused, feeling that God has failed them. And many more begin here to play a pious game of hypocrisy and self-righteousness. Instead of the guilt being removed, the burden of guilt may be only buried deeper where it is left to decay, causing additional suffering. Thousands have then left the church convinced that the church and its God offer no true solution.

Another shortcut route, taken by many, often leaves people confused and still alienated. I can best illustrate by pointing to a couple who came to me for marriage counseling. Mike and Jane were having difficulties that Mike knew were largely of his making. His sense of wrongdoing grew stronger and stronger. His mistreatment of Jane made him feel quite guilty. Trying to deal with his sense of guilt, Mike turned to his pastor and spent much of an afternoon openly confessing his misbehavior. Before God and in the presence of the pastor he wept in sorrow for his failures and for the hurt he had brought to Jane. Mike and the pastor bowed in prayer, asking God to forgive him. He promised himself, his pastor, and God that he was changing that day. Never again would he be such a poor example of a husband. He sealed his commitment with a handshake with his pastor and turned joyfully toward home.

He walked in and announced to Jane that he was a new man and told her that he had talked with the pastor and had prayed for forgiveness and that now all should be well in their marriage. But all was not well. Jane had more than a few choice words to say, and made it clear that she was convinced that he was just up to another of his deceptions. Mike reassured himself that when she saw the change in him over the weeks ahead she would believe him and then all would be well. As the weeks went by, instead of getting better, the relationship only further deteriorated. Mike became confused. He could not understand. He had made himself into a model husband. But Jane continued to stay angry.

When the pastor visited in their home and listened to Jane, he referred the couple to me for marriage counseling. The first session uncovered a major part of the problem. She had been bypassed. It was she who had been insulted many times by her husband. It was she who had been humiliated publicly time and again. It was she who had been slapped during one of his fits of rage a few months before. It was she who had been deeply hurt by his flirtations with some of her friends at a Christmas party. She could go on and on. And where was she at the time he was confessing to the pastor? She was at home crying because she had called his office and someone had laughed and jokingly said that he was probably out with some "cute red-head." Jane knew that he had shown inappropriate interest in a "cute red-head." Although he really had been with the pastor, Jane had been bypassed in his efforts to reconcile. It was she whom he had wounded many times. True reconciliation still needed Jane's forgiveness. He had never confessed – never admitted specific wrongdoing to her. He had never sought her forgiveness.

Before reconciliation can be complete, all parties who have been injured must be dealt with directly. It is often far easier to turn to the God whom we cannot see, admitting our wrong, than to turn to the person in the flesh against whom we have sinned.

Confession demands that we be specific. Many are confused when they find no lifting of their burden of guilt. "I have confessed many times that I have done wrong, but I don't seem to get relief." It is fascinating how often I find, "I have done wrong" is the full extent of the confession. Or one may say, "Of course, I have done wrong. The Bible says that all have sinned and come short of the glory of God. Since I am one of the all, I am a sinner." Evasion of the specific is usually an evasion of the reality of the extent of the wrong and its guilt. Consequently, in continued silence, one holds on to the judgment against the self.

The marriage counselor often sees a version of this problem. "Of course I'm not perfect. But after all, I guess no one is." Only as the individuals involved in the conflict begin to admit wherein they themselves are at fault does anything constructive in the relationship begin to take place. Only when the husband begins to admit that he is failing to meet his obligation to exert leadership in the marriage, or to pick up his socks that he has been throwing down for her to pick up, or to put her ahead of his mother, or when he admits to some other failure – only then can he begin to change. They make progress only as she begins to admit that she is failing to help stay within the family budget -- or that she is flirting with other men to make her husband jealous. They make progress when she admits that she frequently calls mama to get advice on how to get her husband to do the things she wants him to do. Only when they get specific is change possible. Only as they place a finger on their own specific failures do they begin to make constructive changes. And only then can they begin to forgive one another and begin to forgive themselves.

Repentance

To be ready and able to accept forgiveness, one must determine to turn away from previous misbehavior. Just as the will was involved in the turn from the pathway of the constructive life, willful choice is necessarily involved in turning back toward the way of the constructive life. Without the turn from the former behavior toward a new pattern of behavior, there is no repentance; and there can be no true experience of forgiveness. It is unfortunate that repentance has been commonly viewed as only a feeling of sorrow or regret. Such feelings are important, and will usually be instrumental in motivating the change of direction; but these feelings are more accurately defined as "contrition." Repentance is a change of mind and purpose -- a change in behavioral direction.

Contrition is a part of repentance, but the two cannot be equated. I regularly see people who are highly distressed with themselves about their behavior but are not willing to change that behavior. Only when behavior is altered, has a person initiated repentance that is acceptable even to himself. A widespread attitude is often worded, "There is no way that I can accept forgiveness today when I know that I am going to repeat the same behavior tomorrow." (See figure 11)

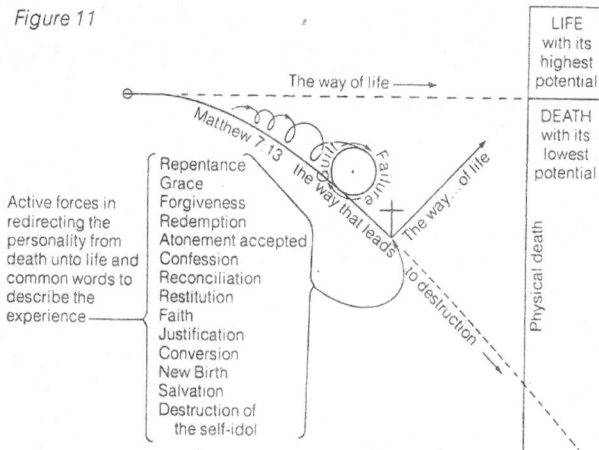

Figure 11

Restitution

Little has been said within Protestant theology concerning the need for restitution. Once again, we are considering a need held by the offender in search of forgiveness of himself. If I have brought harm to another, only when I have done all that I feel is reasonably possible to repair the damage, will I be able to accept forgiveness.   I must make all reasonable efforts to restore to the original owner that which I have taken from him, whether I have taken from his purse, from his reputation, or from his capacity to trust another human being.

The doctrine of meaningful restitution is conspicuously absent from mainstream Christian theology. All too often, well meaning Christians have offered salvation through forgiveness that is uncomplicated by any efforts at meaningful restitution, embarrassment of confession, apology for wrong, sorrow for offenses against others who have been injured, or change in behavior. It is little wonder that theologians Bonhoffer, Mowerer, a large segment of those of the Jewish faith, and many in the world at large have charged Christianity with proclaiming a gospel of "cheap grace." When nothing more is required than walking down the aisle of a church, shaking hands with a preacher, filling out of a 3 x 5 index card, and perhaps attending a few hours of instruction, it sounds like a grace that is unacceptable, unrealistic, invalid, and impotent. Although it may not be a "popular gospel," the gospel of the New Testament calls for a faith commitment and change. It calls for embarrassing confrontation with apologies and restitution.

Let's assume that I have stolen a thousand dollars from you. It is less than meaningless for me to approach you, asking for forgiveness while the money is yet in my pocket and I have every intention of keeping it there for my own use. Even if you should honestly forgive me, not holding it to my indebtedness in any way, I cannot accept forgiveness.

Similarly, let's assume that I have spread a harmful story about you. Whether it is true or untrue is irrelevant. The damage to your reputation may scatter as feathers in the wind, but until I have made every reasonable effort to clear your name, it is meaningless for me to ask you to forgive me. Though you may graciously do so, I cannot yet accept it! Recognizing this as a need of the offender, Alcoholics Anonymous include as step 9 of the 12 steps to recovery, "Make direct amends to such people wherever possible except when to do so should injure them or others."

AA has recognized something that is unrecognized by many churches of the land. AA recognizes that there are times when restitution is impossible or that efforts to make restitution would only compound the damage that has been done already. Consider the man who is living with his third wife at the time he turns to God in repentance from his destructive pattern of life, to a new constructive way. He can only go on from where he is. He cannot disrupt his current marriage relationship, turning his back on all the obligations that go with it. Nor can he go back and make amends to the previous wives for the hurt he brought to them. Effort to do so would only cause fresh injury to them as they now try to build their lives with new families.

Similarly, in the instance of the man who had stolen the thousand dollars. With the money long ago having been spent, actual restitution may bring such hardship to his family that they would suffer greatly by his efforts to repay. He may have to live with his regrets and a dream of restitution in the future.

Faith

Going along with confession and efforts at restitution is the matter of faith. By faith I commit myself to the one to whom I confess. Someone has well said that in the act of confession we fling ourselves into the arms of humanity and God feeling the ever-present possibility of rejection. In confession, I trust myself to the response of the one to whom I confess. I am making myself vulnerable to his attack of criticism and rejection. I take the chance that the person to whom I confess will think as little of me as I think of myself. I leap in faith with the hope and prayer that I will be received with open arms.

It is for this cause that the one hearing confession (the confessor[1]) must be one of great patience. That person must live without a critical spirit. He or she must also be one in whom dwells a spirit of acceptance and additionally, one in whom dwells the Holy Spirit! In the person hearing confession is the power to curse or bless. It was no accident that the ancient Hebrew word for "curse" was the same word as the word for "bless." As we noted in an earlier chapter, only the way the word was used determined the meaning and understanding of it. By accepting the person who is confessing (the confessant) in a spirit of love, the confessor can help to make the act of confession a blessed, healing experience. If, however, the confessant finds rejection, ridicule, or condemnation, the confessor simply adds to the curse of rejection and pushes the guilt-ridden person deeper into his pit of despair. He is given an additional shove down the way of destruction. The confessor, therefore, has a sacred trust to try, with every power of love and acceptance that he can command, to refrain from judgment.

If the confessant finds rejecting judgment, his conclusion is that he has been correct about himself. He feels that he truly deserves damnation. Another person agrees with him—a person in authority. Instead of being closer to reconciliation, he is much farther from it. He tends to accept the condemning attitude of the confessor as the attitude of God and of the society that the confessor represents. The confessant, therefore, approaches the confessor with the hope and prayer that he will be accepted. He comes in faith! Is there any sense in which absolution is made possible

1 The word "confessor" represents one of the many confusing peculiarities of the English language. Merriam-Webster's Dictionary defines the person who hears confession as the confessor, and it also defines the person who confesses as the confessor.

by the confessor? Is there any way for the confessor (the person hearing confession) to set one free from the obligation of guilt? There is indeed! To one who was to hear confession, Jesus said, "Whatever you shall bind on earth shall have been bound in Heaven, and whatever you shall loose on earth shall have been loosed in Heaven" (Mt. 16:19 NASB). The confessor has the responsibility before God to hold up a high standard of conduct by which people can live well on the earth. But that same confessor has a responsibility to convey an attitude of forgiveness that will help the penitent to be released from that which God will have already released him.

While listening intently to a person in the process of openly admitting failings, I spoke of the love of God and of my assurance that she was still acceptable to God.
I told her, "God is willing to forgive you." "But", she said, "Can you forgive me?" I'm a Protestant minister. I sat stunned. She was asking me to forgive her sin. I started to tell her that her wrong was not for me to forgive, but for God to forgive. While I was trying quickly to determine how to answer her, she continued, "Unless you as a human being can forgive me, I feel that only your verbal assurance that God forgives me is beyond my ability to accept." Filled with a sense of awe -- a kind of fear, I responded, "I forgive you. I cannot hold your misconduct to your charge. I still care about you. I still respect you in spite of the bad things you have told me about yourself." With that, she heaved a sigh of relief, "If you can still love me just like I am, then surely God is greater than you. Then He forgives me too."

Chapter 12

We Receive Pardon By Royal Decree

Love is the most healing power on the face of the earth. As hatred is the power of personality destruction, love is the power of personality construction. It is a force – a force that has the potential to change people. With love, God hears the confession of the penitent. He knows the extent of our regret. He understands the humiliation felt in admitting the wrongdoing. He recognizes the faith exercised in the approach to Him with the admission of guilt. He knows the extent of the desire to change by repentance.

At the heart of the Gospel (the Good News) of the Christian message is the truth that God loves us always and is calling us to accept that love. The poet, Francis Thompson, has reverently portrayed Him as the Hound of Heaven in relentless pursuit of fleeing humankind as He tries to get people to accept pardon as His gift of love. Forgiveness is one of the gifts of love that God offers to every person. It is His nature to forgive those who sincerely want it.

Forgiveness

Love, expressed as forgiveness, has the power to set free – to liberate from the anxious expectation of a penalty – to set loose for growth. Forgiveness says, "You are free. You are granted a pardon for the offense you committed. It is no longer held to your charge. There is no resentment felt for you. You are absolved from indebtedness created by your misbehavior and restored to your former status. I remove the barrier called, 'alienation'."

Ancient roots of our word, "forgiveness", mean "to stroke" or "to rub over." Another root means to "lift up and bear away." Hence, we commonly define forgiveness in terms of "covering over," "wiping away," "taking away," or "removing" the barrier. No further debt needs to be paid.

Forgiveness does not "undo" anything. In a moment of rage, Nat swung at his wife. He missed her and hit the refrigerator, breaking two bones and leaving a dent in the door of the freezer compartment. This experience rudely awakened them both. They suddenly realized how far their relationship had eroded. After Nat spent several hours in surgery and the couple spent several months in marital counseling, the two were able to make the necessary adjustments for achieving a beautiful relationship. Although Carol has forgiven Nat for intending to hit her, and he has forgiven himself, the dent remains in the door of the refrigerator, and Nat is still experiencing arthritic complications in the injured hand. He may continue to reap the consequences of his misbehavior for the rest of his life. He may continue to "pay" for having tried to hit her. The physical cause-and-effect results will go unchanged by forgiveness. The change affected in forgiveness is in the interpersonal relationships. By forgiveness, he is no longer obligated to pay her or to pay himself back for having tried to hurt her. Forgiveness eliminates the further eroding of the personality and the further need to make oneself "pay" for misdeeds.

But our own forgiveness also requires that we forgive others. The refusal to forgive requires the carrying of a grudge and the carrying of the grudge damages the carrier. It is only self-defeating and eroding to the personality, which means that when we fail to forgive, we become truly guilty. Deep within, we know that grudge-carrying is against our own best interest. Therefore, it is a sin. Accepting forgiveness while holding to an unforgiving spirit is inconsistent. It equates permitting something to be taken while keeping it. I cannot let you take my car while I still keep it. Nor can I let you take away my debt of guilt while I hold on to my own unforgiving spirit that makes me guilty.

Forgiveness "puts away" any charge against, cancels indebtedness, and clears the record of the offender. Forgiveness says, "Your 'fine' is lifted. You are pardoned." Accepting it says, "I am pardoned -- not let off on account of good behavior, but pardoned."

At the very heart of the Gospel (good news) of Jesus Christ is forgiveness. This is not merely a Biblical doctrine, but a realized experience. In forgiveness, we are blessed. We are freed of the curse placed upon ourselves -- freed of the displeasure from the person we have wronged, and freed of the displeasure of God. We are no longer damned by the little god we made of ourselves. We are blessed by the Majestic God of the Universe. We are accepted. Loved!

Reconciliation

Immediately upon accepting forgiveness, there is a change in the relationships! Forgiveness works toward bringing together relationships alienated by wrongdoing. When relationships have been severed and a gap has been created, forgiveness works to banish the distance between personalities. Alienation that was so keenly felt has disappeared. The distance in the relationship has gone. It has been removed. The barrier between the personalities is torn down and removed.

For true wholeness there must be reconciliation in all planes of relationships; with God, with the important people in our world, and with ourselves. As one is reconciled, therefore, the fragmentation one has pre-viously known begins to heal. The fractured, disintegrated self is becoming whole.

Note that reconciliation made possible by forgiveness, is something the person cannot do for or by himself. If I have wronged you, I cannot remove the barrier I have put up between the two of us. Only the person who has been offended can do the forgiving. God removes the barrier by forgiveness. Therefore, it is He who makes reconciliation possible. He reconciles us to Himself by forgiveness and by our response to His payment by the death of His son (Rom. 5:10).

Being loved so much that my misdeeds are forgiven and are no longer held to my charge before God makes it easier for me to forgive myself. Loving myself (working in my true best interests), I feel no longer the need to pay for my wrongdoing, because Christ has already paid the debt. No longer needing to pay for my misdeeds, I am henceforth freed from the "cycle of the damned." This freedom, in theological terms, is called "redemption." Released from the otherwise endless cycle of the damned, I am "saved."

By forgiveness, I am saved from both the consequences of my own assigned punishment for violation of my own adapted set of law and also from the just judgment of God. I am no longer under the "curse of the law." I am no longer under the curse of my own overly demanding conscience. The law has served as a mirror, reflecting my failure, but because of forgiveness, I am no longer condemned, and I am no longer under its curse. The former self is overcome through change – constructive, observable change permeating (somewhat as yeast in bread) every part of the personality. This change shows itself in our interpersonal relationships.

In years gone by, those who entered into a peaceful, harmonious relationship with God, others, and themselves were said to "have religion." This phrase, filled with meaning, seems to come from two Latin forms. The prefix "re" means "again" and "ligion" coming from "ligare," means "to tie or bind together." Hence "re-ligion" describes that which has been tied or bound together again. Religion is the binding together again the relationship between God and man. They who accept God's grace of forgiveness, becoming reconciled, truly having religion.

Becoming reunited to the God from whom he was earlier separated, he is with God. That is, he is re (again) con (together) ciliated (infused), -- that is he is "reconciled" to God. Their relationship is in harmony. He no longer sees God as an enemy; nor is he God's enemy. Instead of feeling the need to run from God, he walks with God in accord.

Unfortunately, too many stop at this point. To be truly reconciled, harmony must be affected in two other dimensions. Remember that much of the trouble started when the person became at odds with himself. Much of the propelling force in his spiral downward in the cycle of the damned was the hatred he felt for himself.

Reconciled persons not only have accepted forgiveness of God, but they also have forgiven themselves. No longer at war with themselves, they are at peace with themselves. And true peace requires harmony, not only the absence of war. Those who live in harmony with themselves can like the person who lives within their own skin, and eventually are able to develop a healthy self-love. We each need a healthy sense of compassion for ourselves and for others.

But some will want to counter immediately that this is not a good, "Christian" attitude. This concern may arise from the fear that a good image of ourselves will produce an exaggerated sense of pride which will lead to further sin. The word "pride" can refer to a healthy sense of worth, dignity, and self-esteem.

But pride, when it connotes an exaggerated self-esteem, puffs-up one's own virtues and usually minimizes the value of others. It is this attitude the Apostle Paul seems to have in mind when he said, "I say to every man among you not to think more highly of himself than he ought to think, but to think so as to have sound judgment" (Rom. 12:3).

A healthy love for one's self must not be confused with, "being in love with oneself." Those overly "sold on themselves," almost without exception, are using that outer attitude as a mask to conceal their basic contempt for themselves. It is their way of compensating and hiding self-hatred. This will not seem peculiar if we realize that it is normal to want to hide a loathsome creature behind some kind of mask. Of course, we are again discussing the motivation for the trait called "hypocrisy."

Pointing to the need for a healthy self-love, Jesus gave the second greatest commandment; we are to love our neighbor as we love ourselves. (cf. Mt. 36-40). Both while and in the same manner we love ourselves, we are to love our neighbor! Jesus commanded that we work in the true best interests of others while working also in our own true best interests. "Best interests" are those that promote growth toward wholeness. One must acquire a healthy love for himself before he is free to have a healthy love for the other people in his world. And he who is not free to love others is not yet free of self-defeating attitudes and behavior.

The world has seen enough of the "just-me-and-Jesus" per-version of Christianity -- the version acted out as, "let the world be damned. You and I will eat sugar plums and hold hands while we keep folks of other beliefs, other ethnic backgrounds, or other color in 'their place.' We'll overcharge the poor in the name of "shrewd business" and find an excuse to release the older employee a year before retirement. We'll slander the neighbor and abuse the line-worker who is afraid to quit for fear he'll not be able to get another job." And all the while, this character may be mouthing beautiful religious platitudes.

For true reconciliation, one must be at peace with the people of his world, living in a manner that will work toward bringing peace and will work for the highest good of others. And religion that is short of the kind of love that works toward the good of others is short of Christianity as taught by Jesus Christ!

The hypocrite's veil is thin. His deceit rarely fools any but himself and even that works only for a short while. His guilt is there, and deep within, he knows it. In an effort to gain a release from the burden of guilt and its demand for payment, the hypocrite, like many others, may try to "get let off for good behavior." He thinks, "if I act good enough or am generous enough or kind enough, maybe I can "make up" for (balance) the wrong I've done. I will reform! I'll change myself. I'll be such an upstanding, upright, honest, moral person that others will love me, God will love me, and I will even be able to love myself. If I become adequately just in my behavior, I'll gain the love and respect of all who know me."

But some problems eventually arise. How good do I have to be in order to be accepted? How much of me do I have to give to others? How scrupulously honest do I have to be? In my process of self-perfection, how upright must I become to be acceptable? It seems that I hear a faint voice saying, "If you would be perfect, be ye therefore perfect as the Father in Heaven is perfect. (Mt. 5:48). But that's impossible! Then I need something I cannot provide for myself and someone to provide it.

Then, too, if I feel that I have attained the perfection that is demanded, what if I "goof?" What if I fall from that height of sublime achievement of perfection? I can't keep it up forever. Sooner or later I'll fail. What greater anxiety can arise within me? My law will again have become a curse (cf. Ga.l. 3:13). I will have lost my self-earned status. Why fool myself? I'll not make it successfully through the first day. He lies who says that he is always living the best he knows how.

Even if I should make myself perfectly righteous, there is yet another problem. Once I have finally achieved the level of perfection that makes it possible for me to be accepted, my earned acceptance is not registered within me as genuine. I need a genuine love – unconditional love -- acceptance given to me just as I am now, not as I possibly can become.

A less well-known but more apt word is needed in the foregoing paragraphs. The archaic, theological sounding word is "justification." It is also directly related to "righteousness" and "uprightness." In the process of self-justification, one is trying to gain a favorable standing with God, his neighbor, and himself by improving himself. If one is to be justified, that is, if one is to be brought into a favorable standing with God, and himself, he will have to trust God to grant to him that favorable standing. God wants to do for us that which we cannot do for ourselves. He asks that we let Him justify us.

The need for justification is more than some minor doctrine for only the detached, "ivory-towered" theologian to ponder. We are looking at one of the major barriers between a guilty person and his ability to accept forgiveness! A closer, but highly limited study is necessary.

Justification

Let us digress for a moment to review an important matter we considered earlier. While we may confess our personal responsibility, we may, at the same time, make a tragic mistake by trying to justify our behavior. In self-justification, we are essentially rationalizing by saying, "All right, I admit I did as I am accused, but I did so with a just cause. Under the circumstances, I have a legally sufficient reason for my moral failing." Look momentarily at three instances.

Jack lied about Fred. In turn, Fred rationalized that it was only just for him to broadcast an embarrassing truth about Jack.

Larry confided, "My wife is cold and distant. She never puts any feeling into her kisses. She nags me for everything! I'm a man with a man's need for a woman's loving tenderness. It was only natural for me to turn to another woman."

Or the self-justification may come out as Paula expressed it: "I came up poor and was always afraid I'd starve to death. Now I always eat too much."

There is at least one outstanding fallacy in all of these efforts at justification. They are all inadequate and deep inside they know it and the sense of guilt is still there. None of us have the capacity for the depth of personal insight to fully, adequately, justify our failings. We cannot fully satisfy even our own sense of accusation. Deep within, we secretly know that there are other motivations for our behavior, though we cannot quite put our finger on them. No one can!

Let's look closer at each of the examples just cited. When Fred decided to lie in retaliation against Jack, he was unable to see within himself the need to gain a sense of superiority by deflating Jack in the eyes of others. It's what I call the "game of balloon bursting." It's played as follows: if I have a balloon and I see that you have one that is larger, I burst yours so that by comparison mine is big. It can be played by fault-finding in others or by outright lying. If I can make you look little in another's eyes for just a few moments, I can feel bigger by comparison. Not only did Fred have the need to feel superior, there is evidence that he also had the need to reduce himself. He knew that by trying to deflate Jack's image in the eyes of others, he was later going to think less of himself for having done so; and others would think less of him too. These are only a few of the subtle motivating needs in Fred's behavior that he did not have the ability to see within himself at the time. His efforts at self-justification for his spreading of lies were, therefore, totally inadequate!   And somewhere just below his level of conscious awareness, he knows it!

The motivating forces within Larry are equally subtle. Remember that Larry was justifying his marital infidelity by blaming his wife's coldness and nagging, and by his claims of having a strong need for a woman's tenderness. But Larry also has the need to make his wife suffer the pain of feeling rejected. He also finds it flattering to get another woman interested in him. She'll not satisfy him. As soon as he feels he has won her, he will no longer want her. He will need to move on to another. In this manner he can prove his masculinity to himself. He minimizes his secret doubts about his own masculinity and gets some reassurance each time he conquers another woman. At the same time, he can satisfy his need to hurt one woman after another. He gets secret satisfaction in knowing they are emotionally wounded by his departure. This makes him feel powerful. All of the hurt he inflicts upon his wife and others fulfils his need to pay by degrading himself more and more. All of these and many more subtle motivations for his behavior are somewhere below his conscious awareness as he tries to justify himself. He cannot see himself adequately to justify himself fully. Nor can he ever do so.

Paula tried to justify her extreme obesity by saying that she had always feared she might starve. This may have been true, but her justification was incomplete. At this time she cannot remember that the first time she cleaned her plate, as a small child, her mother praised her. That was the first approval she ever felt from her mother. At the next meal she cleaned her plate and received praise again. Throughout her entire childhood, the only praise she ever received from her mother was for eating all of her food. As a fat adult, each time she cleared her plate she heard an old echo that praised her. Long after her mother's death, she could still hear a voice of approval following each meal. Wait. We have not heard all of Paula's secret motives for carrying excessive weight.

When Paula was in her late teens, with the encouragement of a concerned physician, she went on a diet and lost more than one hundred fifty of her three hundred pounds. With determination and the praise of her doctor and friends, she was sure she would achieve the goal of one hundred twenty five pounds.

However, a new problem appeared. With the loss of so much weight, she was becoming quite attractive. Boys had rarely noticed her before, except to make a passing remark that painfully reminded her of her excessive weight. Going out with young men stirred her sexual drives that made self-control difficult when they made advances. She was feeling guilty for even letting herself feel a desire for erotic gratification. When she eventually yielded to a young man's seduction, she felt degraded and dirty. Feeling that one time was as bad as fifty, she decided that she may as well abandon restraints. After several men and mountains of guilt, she remembered that she had never had such problems when she was fat. None of her friends could understand why such a pretty girl would let herself gain weight again. It took her only a year to put on one hundred pounds. Since men in our culture generally are less interested in extremely obese women, her problem of how to deal with their seductive efforts and her own erotic desires was solved. She joined the thousands of others who are motivated to obesity by the same kind of struggle. I have heard it too many times in the counseling office to believe otherwise. Until she learns to deal more constructively with her aroused passions, she will maintain her weight through diet after diet.

Paula's earlier efforts to justify her overeating were inadequate. And she ultimately may still have more subtle motivations which she will not yet have faced. Among them may be her need to slowly destroy herself with food for some of her misbehavior. Deeper and deeper study of her would reveal more and more hidden motives. She does not have the capacity to fully justify herself for lack of full self-knowledge. It must be repeated that we never know ourselves well enough to fully justify ourselves. No amount of psychotherapy, or counseling, or anything else will ever be adequate for total self understanding.

Only God can know any person's motivating drives well enough to justify totally. God does for us what we cannot do for ourselves! Those who are still trying to justify themselves are not fully accepting God's justification of them. They still are trying to hide their real guilt; and in doing so, they are denying themselves the privilege of experiencing forgiveness. As long as we are trying to justify ourselves, we do not accept God's justification of us. We admit little for which forgiveness is needed. We are right when we admit that we have been wrong.

God comes to us saying, "Instead of wasting your time and effort trying to justify yourself, surrender, trusting me to justify you. You are not as upright (right or correct) as you want to see yourself to be, but I love you anyway. I see your true motivations for what you do and I still love you."

When I saw that I was loved just as I am, something "clicked" inside. Something happened. Something seemed to die. Something of *me* seemed to die. But what was it? My self-hatred! If I am loved by the Creator of the universe, why should I hate myself any longer? Loved, I no longer have the need to hate myself. I no longer have the need to slowly destroy myself. I then, also, lost the need to pay for my own sins. If I no longer need to pay for my own sins, the "cycle of the damned" is broken. God has set me free – redeemed me from the destructive "cycle of the damned."

But something in me has been destroyed! God did it with His love. He destroyed my need to destroy myself. My personality has undergone a major change! I am transformed! I am set free! As the former me was dying, a new me was coming forth.

A counselee once told me of this experience while it was happening. In my office, she had decided to trust Christ as the Lord of her life and to accept His transforming work in it. While we talked, seeming somewhat startled, she said, "As I watch me die, I have the feeling that a new little baby me is taking shape right here in the region of my heart." With excitement, she added, I know it sounds crazy, but I have the distinct impression that I am just now being born!" There it is! After her heart having pumped and having breathed for half a century, and having been in the process of dying for nearly as long, she was being born anew; not of the flesh, but of the Spirit; not of her will, but of the will of God (cf. John 1:12-13).

We have to die before we can truly live. While we yet walk on the face of the earth, our zoe – our spiritual life will die – either from our own degenerative efforts or in preparation for the regenerative work of God.

Destroying the Idol

Since men have a lifetime struggle with their efforts to "be as God," we must look again at the problem of idolatry. When we have earlier succeeded at self-deification, it ought not to seem strange that we should think it necessary to die. Any god that is dethroned is almost always destroyed! History reveals, again and again, that when idol gods are torn down, they usually are destroyed. We get angry when we see how foolish we have been. We don't want reminders of that foolishness left around. We feel the idol should be destroyed, even if the idol that has been worshiped is our self – we have to die!

Then too, the former god must be done away with before another god can be given full allegiance. No man can have two ultimate authorities in his life. It is unfortunate that the atheist is often rejected or ridiculed by followers of organized religions. Men live by the adage; "Show me a God and I'll worship Him." The only god the atheist recognizes is himself. But, as we've said before, denial is one of the most commonly used defense mechanisms of humankind. And the atheist's denial of the reality of God is, in large part, his defense. Total denial is less embarrassing and otherwise confronting than open admission that one is secretly a god in and of himself.

There is little difference in professed atheism and practicing atheism. The former may verbally deny the existence of a deity, whereas the practicing or practical atheist admits that a God exists somewhere, but his life-style gives no allegiance to any god (beyond himself). In both persons lives the practicing attitude, "I'll do it my way. I'm all-wise. I know what's best for me. I'm the authority." (Translated, that means, "I'm my own god.)"

Such an ego state is difficult to surrender. But men do it daily. Though I have no quarrel with the Christian theologian Bonhoeffer's position that obedience is a cost of discipleship, the ultimate cost of discipleship is the surrender of one's own self-image as deity. James Emmerson wrote:

The real cost of discipleship is to accept forgiveness -- and that is a genuine sacrifice. It means that a man must surrender his god-centeredness about himself, his ego, his all to the true God (p.73). When the god one has made of himself dies, new life emerges.

Once again, let's return to the progression of line illustrations. Back in chapter 6 the weakening, deteriorating self was represented as caught in a "snowballing" cycle of the damned – a cycle of failure and guilt, "hell-bent for destruction." (Fig. 9) The future seemed only dark. The news was only bad. But God declared, "I have now given you a choice between a blessing and a curse . . . the choice between life and death" (Deut. 30:1 & 19 TEV). You choose! If the choice is LIFE, the future is bright.

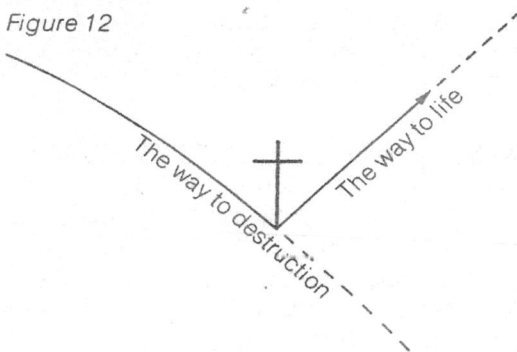

Figure 12

Study Figure 12 in light of all that has been said thus far in this book.

The Apostle Paul wrote, "If any man be in Christ he is a new creature, old things are passed away, behold, all things are become new" (I Cor. 5:17). Paul recognized that virtually everything in life is changed in its direction when one chooses a new life in relationship with God through Jesus Christ. Whereas, "the wages of sin is death, . . . the gift of God is eternal life" (Rom. 6:23). With new life, one is a new creature; a newly created being who no longer must see himself, in one instant, a god to be adored and in the next instant, a devil to be despised. He is now a new person slowly growing toward his life's highest potential.

However, before we look at these changes, we must point to some of the limitations. No matter how total the recreation, some damages done along the way can never be reversed. We earlier had to make a similar statement about forgiveness. The repentant alcoholic may have destroyed three marriages, taught six children to hate him, destroyed his liver and he may have helped to drag several other people into his pit. He cannot suddenly "undo" all the damage. He may be truly repentant. He may be recreated by the redemptive miracle of God, and he may have a new life ahead of him, but the damages to his physical body, to the marriages, and to his children will not be erased. They will remain as scars and painful reminders of where he has been.

A noted religious leader of the early Christian era was directly responsible for the pain and suffering of many who followed the way of Christ. Evidence suggests that he even may have been responsible for the death of some. When that man, Saul, was changed (converted) by the re-creative miracle of God, he took a new name, Paul. But he had to live with the painful, haunting memories of his misdeeds. And his victims still carried their scars.

Some students of Biblical history think these painful memories may have been Paul's "thorn in the flesh" of which he wrote (cf. II Cor. 12:7).

Thousands now live with the painful memories of their own misdeeds, but they also live in the joy of renewal. Through repentance and the re-creative work of God, they have turned away from the path of destruction to a new direction. The new direction is toward LIFE. It is a life affirming, life asserting, life fulfilling way. It is the way toward life's highest potential -- toward the highest sense of realization. It is toward maturity to the fullest dimension. It is this redirection toward life that the early church called "the way", suggesting both direction and movement. When compared to the former behavior and attitudes of the man who was entrapped in the cycle of the damned, there will be observable differences in the reconciled man as he continues in the process of becoming the person God intended him to be.

As, "all things are becoming new," for the "new creature," he begins to realize that his new love for God, his new love for others, and his new love for himself give him a new purpose. Dr. Victor Frankl has called attention to the fact that for one to really live, he must have a purpose for his existence. He must justify to himself a purpose for occupying space on planet Earth. With no purpose outside himself, he becomes miserable, with a sense of worthlessness, boredom, and futility (pp.154ff). Jesus Christ provides a purpose.

Jesus taught that if a man is to find himself, he can do so when he loses himself in service for His sake and for the purposes of the Gospel (Lk. 9:26). The desire to serve is one of the gifts of grace from God. Out of love, God gives what men need! God provides it as he instllls in the regenerate heart the desire to serve other human beings. The individual must look to God for leadership to find how and where he can best serve.

Observe these who serve: some as nurses, some as sweepers of floors, some as homemakers, and some dig ditches working to provide for their families. While providing for their own needs, they seek to give something of themselves to others around them.

After some of His followers had fed the hungry, had given water to the thirsty, had given refuge to a stranger, and dressed one in need of clothing, had visited the sick and had befriended the imprisoned, Jesus said that these good works had been done unto Him (Mt. 25:35ff). He seems to be speaking in the same manner that I would, concerning anyone who befriends my wife, my children, or my friends who may be in need. In a very real sense, anyone who helps those I love, does something good for me. If you express love to them, you express love for me. Service to those whom God loves is a service to God.

Much more is new on "The Way." We can experience new growth; and in fellowship with God in Christ, we may always know that the best is yet to be. I am not yet what I have the potential to become, and the same can be said by anyone on "The Way" up from out of the depths of self-destruction. I reemphasize this point for those who may have the impression that the repentant become perfect immediately upon appeal to God for forgiveness and recreation.

Consider the man who had been quite profane and crude in his language. Five minutes after having first accepted God's redeeming love, he bowed in a joyous prayer of thanksgiving. "Thank you God for savin' me from myself. I need help. I'm tired. I'm tired of the way I been actin'. I'm expectin' you to help me change the half-ass way I been treatin' people." Crude? Yes. But he is on the way up with more concern for his relationship with people than with a bit of back alley verbiage. He is not yet what he can become in the way he acts toward people or in the language he uses.

With each recognized stage of growth and with each improvement in behavior, there is a new sense of worth. The person's dignity as a human being is in process of being restored. The person is "becoming" -- that is, the person is becoming more of a person, with even a deepening capacity for faith.

Obedience as Faith

The word "faith" conveys the idea of "confidence" or "trust" and can mean "belief in" a person or principle. For a more accurate and more complete understanding of the word, we have to include "obedience" to make the concept of "faith" more complete.

Obedience says, "I trust you enough to believe you want what is best for me, therefore, I will do as you bid, surrendering myself to your leadership." As in the incident related in an early chapter concerning my children and the poison ivy, the children expressed faith in me by staying away from the poison ivy, as I had asked. Obedience was their way of saying, "I trust daddy's concern for my well-being enough to do as he asks. I do not know by experience that the poison ivy will harm me. He is older and more experienced. He loves me. If he says that for my benefit I ought to stay away from it, that's good enough for me. I'll submit to his leadership. I'll do as he asks." Their obedience to my instruction to stay away from the poison ivy demonstrated their faith in me.

Someone may ask, "But what of the element of fear?" Yes, the Bible says that the fear of the Lord is the beginning of wisdom, but the word fear here means "intense reverence or awe." In the experience with our children, they knew fear also – the kind of fear that threatens harm. Their faith in me had caused them to fear the poison. They believed me! They were not frightened of me, but they feared the natural consequences of touching the poison ivy. In a similar way, we need not be frightened of God, but we do well to be frightened of the natural consequences of our behavior that is disobedient to Him.

When Lisa, our daughter, was roughly four years old, she teetered on the arm of a rocking chair, wildly rocking back and forth. I asked her to stop. When she continued as though I had not spoken I repeated by request. Still rocking, she said impatiently, "Daddy, I'm not going to get hurt." I thought, "All right, Honey. I'll just have to leave you to learn the hard way, by experience." Before I could speak in response to her statement, she flipped backward and bumped her head when she hit the heavily carpeted floor. She rolled about the floor, crying. I said nothing, but picked up the newspaper and sat down to read. A few minutes later she lifted the bottom of the paper, crawled into my lap, and snuggled comfortably while I quietly petted her. After a few minutes, she looked up and said, "Daddy, you want what is best for me, don't you?" That's the point! A Heavenly Father, by His limitless knowledge and the experience of countless centuries, knows what is best for us, His children. He asks that we trust Him enough to obediently follow His leadership. He forces no one to follow it.

Obedience to the "Ought" of God

By obedience to God, we are talking about living up to the "ought." Not just any "ought," but the "ought" of God. The Creator of the universe knows fully what behavior is most constructive for His children.

Since God does not speak as man, we may wonder how to know His leadership. It will best be sought in two directions: the Bible and in prayer. The Bible is largely an historical account of ordinary men living their lives in the day by day ordinary events. Though usually considered a "sacred" book, it is as secular as a woman sweeping her house, fishermen casting their nets to earn their livelihood, and a man "down on his luck," having lost everything he had. It is as secular as a business man stealing from his customers, sailors throwing goods overboard while trying to survive a storm at sea, and a top government official scheming and plotting the death of one of his own soldiers in battle so that he could take the widow for himself. Through hundreds of other everyday events, God communicated truths to men about how they ought to live and relate with Him and with one another. From each of these events we can learn better how to conduct ourselves so that we, and others around us, may fare better in this pilgrimage called Life.

If I had suspected that I would not be around to clearly teach my children during their formative years, I would have written some words of encouragement and instruction that I would have hoped they would follow, so that they might enjoy a more abundant life. I had learned some things that I would have believed they would profit by hearing. Indeed, as I lived with them from day to day, I often expressed some guiding principle. Love required it!

God, as a loving Father, knew that most of us would have a hard time understanding his efforts to teach us in the day to day events of life. He, therefore, gave us the Bible, containing those basic principles needed as we go about the day to day business of living. But those are accounts of events and people from many centuries long gone. Men experience things today that have no parallel in the Bible. Is there some condensed statement of God's primary leading principle that takes into account all the possible circumstances for any person in any era? Yes, and many books could be written on this one subject. Jesus said, ". . . you shall love the Lord your God with all your heart, and with all your soul, and with all your mind. This is the great and foremost commandment. And a

second is like it. You shall love your neighbor as yourself"
(Matt. 22:37-39). There it is once again – the law of
love. To abide by this law one must ask again and again,
"By God's leadership, in this instance, what does love
require?" Recall that this form of love habitually works
in the best interests of those around us. It is important,
therefore, that we try to become aware of the leadership
of God in our present experience, here and now. The
living, resurrected Christ desires to commune with us
as individual persons. He encourages us to participate
with Him in a dialogue called prayer.

Jesus gave a model in his effort to teach us to pray.
(Matt. 6:15). This prayer of Jesus, familiarly known as
"The Lord's Prayer", is indeed a model. He gave it only
as an example and warned against "vain repetition."
Familiarity can breed contempt, even for a prayer – to
the extent that we may recite the words without ever
considering the meaning of what we are saying.

Remember that prayer is basically a two-way
conversation. God invites us to speak our concerns and
interests, but he asks also that we listen. When I was
ministering as a professional hospital chaplain, I talked
with more than 1,000 people each month. Many of my
patients asked me how to pray. I suggested that they
talk to God exactly the same way they talk with anyone
that they highly respect. Many people think it necessary
to pray in the archaic language of the 1611 King James
Version of the Bible. The language itself is not important.
God understands all the utterances of humankind! No
special language has to be learned. Speak with what
you've got. Then listen.

Don't expect a booming roar from Heaven. Don't even
expect an audible voice. He'll speak to your mind. He
will offer leadership and instruction by His use of your
own thought processes. The "still, small voice" ever so

gentle and quiet will be heard in the inner recesses of the heart, so clear one might ask, "Was that really from God or did it originate solely from within my own mind? And there seems to be no way to know for certain.

The skeptic may laugh at the thought of the Creator of the universe actually hearing, much less speaking to mere human beings. Even those who experience such communication may question the experience and admit the possibility that it is entirely subjective. But they will go on to add that when they follow these leading "impulses," both they and others benefit. People are led to serve. And those who serve others do a greater service to themselves. They testify that during and after prayer burdens are lighter, problems have fresh solutions, and peculiar coincidences "happen" which mathematical odds would declare "impossible." Examples rarely persuade. They usually add to the bias of the believer and raise more questions for the skeptic.

We must admit that sometimes one may be mistaken. All instruction thought to be by the leadership of God should be evaluated in light of principles taught in the New Testament. If direction is of God, it will be in keeping with the teachings of His written word as preserved in the New Testament. This is highly important because men have committed terrible crimes against humanity believing they are obeying the "voice of God." From age to age the same, God will not lead one to behave in a manner inconsistent with his written Word. His principles are always leading to the constructive, uplifting benefit of human beings. They thrust men toward the building of life.

Faith vs. Legalism

Webster defines legalism as, "conformity to a code of deeds as a means of justification." By conforming, one attains acceptance. I am not suggesting a new

Legalism. Legalism says, "If you obey enough, you will be acceptable." The obedience that the Bible calls for has a different purpose. The value is found in the individual act that benefits the other person and/or the self. If no other person is involved, my obedience and righteousness is an act that benefits me. Some want to forget the dictionary and insist that legalism is obedience to God simply because God has declared that an act should be performed. If I were to follow that definition, then I would concede that I am a legalist. I am confident that living more than three quarters of a century has given me some wisdom and knowledge to recognize what is likely to be beneficial or harmful to my children. A loving Heavenly Father who has watched human behavior for many thousands of years ought to have infinitely more wisdom and knowledge than I. Even if such wisdom were not a part of His essential nature, He would have attained it as a result of His experience. With that in mind and in the confidence that He wants only the best for me, and others around me, I insist upon obedience as an act of faith.

Fear of Submission

Some resist submitting to God's leadership fearing the loss of their individuality. But it does not follow that each recreated personality will become a carbon copy of another. Each person is an individual as different as one leaf on a grape-vine is different from every other leaf. Only by a casual glance do they appear to be alike. Close examination reveals that each is truly unique; no two are identical. But they are each from the same vine. Each gains nourishment, strength, and life from the same source. Herein lies at least a part of the truth Christ was teaching when he referred to himself as the "true vine" and to his followers as the "branches." (Jn. 15:5)

Nor does submission to divine leadership require us to become as wooden puppets. While surrender to divine leadership calls for commitment, it is commitment only to leadership and not to manipulation. His purpose is to help us to become persons. We retain our own wills. Remember that it was away from becoming persons that we had been moving as we worked to destroy ourselves. It is to the becoming of persons that God calls every person! We will not lose our own personality – our identity. It is to unique humanity – to individualization that he calls. It is to the elevation above the animal and the development of the highest human qualities that He is calling.

I have observed another cause for resistance to submission to a cosmic Father. For many people, the word "father" is almost synonymous with, hate, greed, brutality, selfishness, manipulation, criticism, condemnation, and all else that brings pain. To them, the thought of submitting to the will of any "father" is intolerable. Having known only a pain-inflicting father, some find it almost impossible to believe that a Heavenly Father would really care, wanting only the best for His children. One who has been cursed by the earthly father, finds it difficult to accept the blessing of the Heavenly Father. But the blessing of God saves life, and obedience to Him brings growth. The change is often dramatic.

Salvation as an Experience That Initiates a Process

This change is a revitalizing, rebuilding experience that begins at a point in time and continues progressively. Whereas the personality formerly was in the process of a slow *dis*integration, by the combined efforts of the individual and the help of God, the personality is in process of *re*integration. Instead of becoming more animal-like, the individual is in process of becoming more and more truly human -- more God-like -- more restored to the image of God. One is in process of becoming a true person. He is being re-created. He is becoming more whole. The recovering person is being healed. That is the important word.

The words, "heal," "health," "whole," "holy," and "hale," all come from a common root which meant "complete." The person becoming recreated is becoming more complete. Each day sees him more than he was, but not yet who he has the potential to become. The basic Greek word for the concept of "the process of becoming complete, or being made whole," is sozo.

Let's patiently wade through some of the complexities of this highly important word. Though the New Testament Greek word sozo is most commonly translated "save," it is used many times to indicate "curing" or "healing" as one would "save from an illness." The same word was sometimes used in old literature to mean "to pardon." A form of this word sozo is used in Mark 5:23 to indicate physical (bodily) healing. In Luke 6:36, a form of the word sozo indicates that which some have interpreted as an emotional (mental) healing, and in Luke 1:68 a form of the word sozo is used to indicate religious healing. Jesus is often referred to as the Soter (the Savior who heals, making human beings whole.) From the same root as sozo comes soteria, sometimes translated in the New Testament as "health," though more often it is translated "salvation."

Further study more clearly indicates the experience of "salvation" as a total re-creative process that includes the physical, emotional and spiritual dimensions of the healing experience.

Although sozo sometimes refers to an ongoing process with future implications, in the old Greek world it often denoted an acutely dynamic act in which men were snatched by force from serious peril.

Salvation As An Experience

It is this acutely dynamic act in which God, through the living Christ, snatches men from serious peril. Evangelical Christianity usually calls it "salvation." The 'snatching" concept, from both Biblical and non-Biblical usage of the word sozo, clearly portrays God in objective action working in man's behalf. This "snatching" -- this "turning-point" -- this "redirection" -- this "new birth" -- this "regeneration" was illustrated in a previous chapter (figure 11) to show the turn from death to life.

For your convenience, I am again inserting figure 12 which is a portion of figure 11.

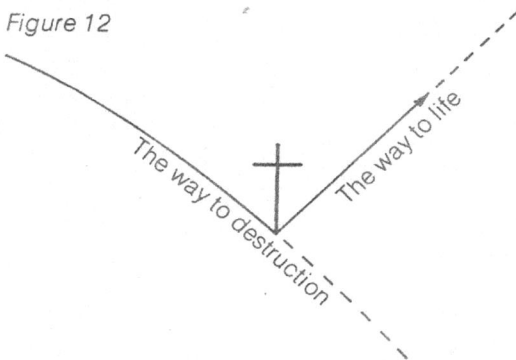

Figure 12

Salvation from destruction ahead was by the action of God. The cause is God alone (by grace), but faith is the channel through which grace is mediated to man.

Because "salvation" carries with it the idea of "ongoing action," some have concluded that one is saved gradually. Not at all! The word conveys instantaneous action - a moment, perhaps known only to God. But it does have an ongoing dimension. Since the word sozo (save) also relates to physical healing, consider a somewhat similar, but limited, parallel in the following example.

Suppose a man, sick with pneumonia, is rapidly getting sicker and sicker, moving toward death. His body is degenerating. Then a strong antibiotic drug is given. He is "saved," (turned back or snatched) from death by the intervening action of the antibiotic; and he is continuing to be saved (being saved) by its influence upon the body as the healing processes continues. The inner-working of the medicine "saves" him from being turned back toward death. An initiating event and a process are roughly illustrated in figures 12 and 13. Observe the similarities. Figure 12 represents the spiritual saving work of Christ. Figure 13 represents the physical saving work of the medicine.

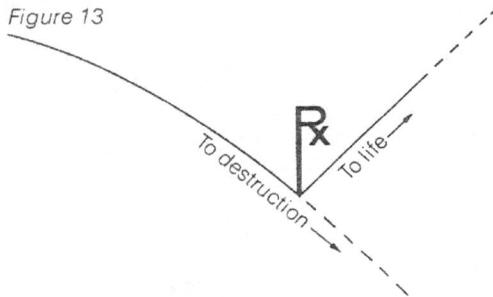

Figure 13

Salvation as Process

Since a process is not the same as a starting event, salvation as a process and salvation as a starting *event* are traditionally shown to be different, with the word "sanctification" referring to the process. There's nothing wrong with this archaic theological word but it seems to have lost meaning in our day. A person in the process is being sanctified (being saved) -- in the sanctification process.

Previously, we have often used the words "degeneration" and "disintegration" to describe the process of tearing apart of the personality. Now, the word "reintegration" seems appropriate to refer to that part of regeneration (salvation) that becomes a process of making whole. The word "reintegration" here further denotes the process of renewal – the opposite of the degenerative process that has been already discussed in earlier chapters (chapters 4,5,&6). Diminishing humanity? No longer! The process of erosion is reversed by the re-creative miracle of the unearned favor of God. It is not something the person has to do or can do entirely by himself. He has the aid of the Original Creator who is a glad, willing Helper in the re-creative process, by the power of the resurrected, living Christ.

Recall the diminishing pie (Chapter 4, Figure 7) which illustrated the steady deterioration of the human personality, becoming less and less human-like – less and less God-like. Figure 14 illustrates a personality in the reversed constructive process of change. By the power of God's love, the personality that has been in a process of disintegration enters into a process of re-integration. Rebuilding of personhood has begun. This is a reconstruction of the personality.

Figure 14

Figure 14 roughly illustrates the recovery of one's true humanity. Though we have repeatedly alluded to the damage to one's humanity, some may still contend that human beings are simply another form of animal. It is more than philosophical to declare that while man is, indeed, an animal, he is more. He is set apart as unique largely on the basis of certain characteristics which include his capacity for abstract and moral judgments. Physically he is unique on the basis of the size of his neocortex – the largest and most dominant part of the brain where abstract and moral judgments reside.

Such judgments determine how we shall act. That which works in any way against man's capacity for moral judgments works against man's basic humanity. Conversely, when his capacities for moral judgments become more complete, the person becomes more complete.

One of the richest words of Hebrew language is the word "shalom." Though commonly translated "peace," it suggests completeness of personality in spirit, emotion, and body. It is by the efforts of Jehovah working through the person of Jesus Christ that a person can enter into the experience of shalom and soteria (peace and salvation) in all of its dimensions. It is by the ongoing re-creative work of the Soter (Savior) that men can become more and more complete.

The more complete we become, the stronger we become. Whereas in former times the person represented by the first "pie-man" (Chapter 4, Figure 7) was becoming weaker and less able to withstand temptation, the person is now becoming stronger and is, therefore, more able to withstand the temptations that would otherwise lead to destructive behavior and attitudes. All of this reversal, renewal, and strengthening is possible because we are not left on our own. We have help (sozo).

Our word sozo has shown up once again. In both Biblical and non-Biblical literature the word is used repeatedly to mean, "to come to the help of." A part of God's saving work in the life of the Christian is in His giving of help along the way, "delivering" and "preserving."

The person of the Holy Spirit of God becomes a constant companion. He moves in, taking up residence within the individual at the time of the new birth (salvation) experience. Both Jesus and the Apostle Paul repeatedly referred to this phenomenon in the life of the Christian. Jesus identified Himself with human beings who were either rejected or neglected. The Apostle Paul said clearly that the body of the Christian is a temple of the Holy Spirit.

With the Spirit of God as a resident companion, the person in process of recreation can expect a greater inclination toward that which is constructive and beneficial to others and to the self. This Spirit of God, also called the Holy Spirit, is totally opposed to the workings of the Satanic Tempter. As it is the desire of the Tempter to dissuade from that which was constructive and beneficial, it is a desire of the Holy Spirit to persuade toward the good and righteous – toward the constructive and beneficial. He encourages toward the virtuous lifestyle for the purpose of bringing constructive benefit to others around us and to ourselves.

Whereas the Satanic Unholy Spirit (the Accuser) tries to strip the individual of his sense of worth and dignity, the Holy Spirit of God encourages and helps the individual behave in such a way as to gain his correct, healthy sense of worth as a person.

With each righteous act, and with each constructive effort extended toward another or toward the self, the Holy Spirit approves and encourages by praise. In the Scriptures, He is sometimes called "the Comforter," but that title does not infer that He is one who makes comfortable. Instead, He is the one who strengthens. "The Comforter" is hence, "The Strengthener," giving strength by encouragement! When we are in process, obedient to the "ought" of God, we are encouraged by the Spirit of God. He says, in effect, "Hey, you have done something beneficial for another and, therefore, it is beneficial for you. Congratulations! You are doing well. You have an attitude that is constructive. Your behavior is character-building. Well done!"

All of God's judgment is not negative, nor is it reserved only for a "Grand Judgment Day" out there somewhere after we have died. When we are doing right, somewhere during this process, the Christian begins to get the message. "I'm succeeding! I'm living up to the correct, beneficial oughts." Our sense of approval is being reinforced. We stand in the positive, affirming judgment of God -- and of ourselves.

Is this to suggest that God is on the sideline or in the stands somewhere only applauding? Not at all! He is in the midst of the experience with us. God's imparted strength to the Christian makes us more inclined to obey -- so much so we will have to exert effort in order to go against the imparted inclination toward righteousness (right, constructive behavior). He prompts toward righteousness and further strengthens by encouragement, which makes it easier to act constructively the next time.

Take note: each time we do that which is in keeping with our sense of "ought," we are encouraged. When encouraged, we feel stronger and enjoy a greater sense of worth and dignity. Thus encouraged, we find it easier to do as we ought the next time.

A cycle is established!
When we are obedient to our sense of "oughtness," the Spirit of God himself "pats us on the back," saying, "You are doing well. Keep it up." We feel encouraged. With such encouragement, we are stronger and more determined to try to continue to please Him and ourself. We tend again to do that which is beneficial and constructive. Our behavior is acceptable to God and to us. We have moved into the "Cycle of the Blessed." It tends to be repeated again and again and again, steadily moving upward. There is obviously a new future in store, for both this side of the grave and the other.

Whereas the "Cycle of the Damned," discussed in Chapter 6 (Figure 9), progressed downward toward destruction, the "Cycle of the Blessed" progresses upward toward that which is more and more constructive and beneficial to the personality. In this process we are the recipients of God's soteria (God's Salvation). But this word that keeps reappearing is also to be translated "blessing," in the form of recovery. It moves us toward that which is emotionally, physically, and spiritually healthful. It moves steadily upward toward fulfillment, toward satisfaction, toward joy, toward contentment, toward enrichment of personality, and toward a better quality of life.

The "cycle of the blessed" goes round and round, up and up, and has the potential for going on and on and on and on eternally. That will be Heaven. See Figures 15 and 16. Figure 15 is the enlarged image represented by the upper right circle in Figure 16.

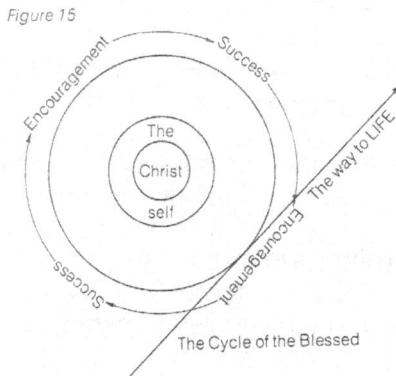

Figure 15

The Cycle of the Blessed

Figure 16

(HEAVEN)
ultimate
LIFE
with its
highest
potential

ultimate
DEATH
with its
lowest
potential
(HELL)

"...the gate to hell is wide and
the road that leads to it is easy,
and...many travel it. But the gate
to life is narrow and the way that
leads to it is hard, and there are
few people who find it."
Matt. 7:13-14 (TEV)

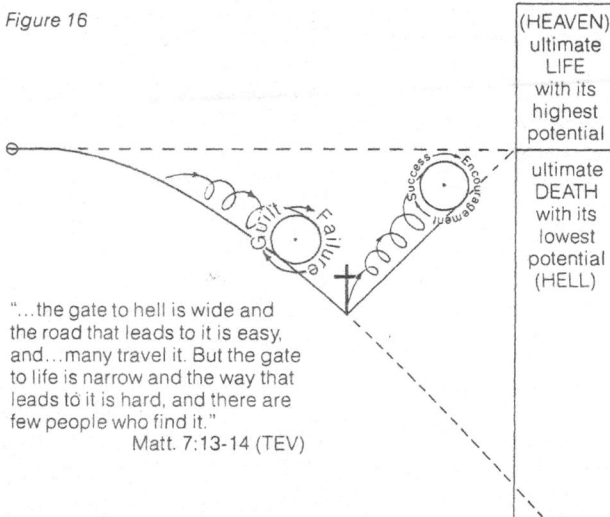

Potential Dangers

In this growth process in the cycle of the blessed, there
is a grave danger of developing an attitude of self-
righteousness! To God be the glory! The glory due is
for God, not for us. One may forget that he is achieving
growth only because he is experiencing the daily
forgiveness, encouragement, and strengthening of God.
Without it one would again become bound by the sense
of failure for occasional violations of the "ought."

Another warning: We must beware of "presuming on
relationships." For example, any husband or wife who
presumes that all in the relationship will automatically
continue well is headed for trouble in a marriage. A
relationship is comparable to a living organism that
must be attended to, or it will get sick. It is rarely static.
If a relationship is not improving it is getting worse. If
both the husband and the wife fail to examine their
relationship regularly, and make efforts to improve
themselves and the way they act toward one another,

their relationship will tend to deteriorate. I've seen it proven hundreds of times in my marriage counseling office.

In a similar way, any person who enters into a trusting, love relationship with God, in Jesus Christ, but neglects the relationship, is headed for trouble. Some of the meanest, most cantankerous, gossipy, vindictive human beings on the face of the earth claim Christianity as their religion. But their attitude and behavior runs counter to the principle of love that the way of Christ demands. They evidence having turned from grace to a new set of "Ten Commandments" (give or take a few) to which they adhere tenaciously, while they could care no less for the people they harm. None came more heavily under the judgment of Jesus, during the days of His flesh, than did the religious hypocrites whom Jesus likened to whitewashed tombs – clean on the outside but inwardly filled with death and corruption. They were not righteous simply because they professed a particular moral ethical code.

For the thief and the prostitute, Jesus expressed compassion and mercy, but to the legalistic self-righteous hypocrite, He expressed scorn, impatience, and warning of harsher judgment to come.

It is easy to lose sight of the fact that each person outside true fellowship with God is living in sin. Since the concept of a general state of sin is too abstract for most of us, we tend to limit it to a list of particular sins. The tendency of some who call for righteousness is to try to make the hearer feel guilty for purely personal sins that leave untouched the questions of overall attitudes toward others, toward one's self, and toward God. The evangelistic thrust has too often emphasized the sins generally catalogued by the Puritans; such as, profane language, dancing, theatrical production, smoking, immoral books, profanation of the Lord's Day, the drinking of alcoholic beverage, and immodest dress. While these indeed may be sins, they do not adequately relate to the total life. And undue preoccupation with them permits the self not to notice the vast realms of human relationships where sin may run unchecked.

Such an effort to create guilt feelings about such specific sins can bring about a spurious conversion. Hubert McAvoy appropriately expressed this concern:

There is real danger that a mere feeling of release, sometimes bringing some mastery over a particular catalogue of sins to be sure, but not a vital, experience changing the life may be induced by a process of self-hypnotism. This kind of thinking ignores the Christian doctrine stressing a growth in grace. It vitiates (makes weak) any notion of sanctification (growth) as a process under the guidance of the Holy Spirit, and tends to make the individual feel that his entire salvation is accomplished -- repentance, acceptance, and sanctification, all in one fell swoop. His feeling of the moment rules him and not his increasing experience of the grace of God effectively operative in all areas of his life. The conversion is not an objective fact in his total life observable to others, but a subjective feeling known only to himself. This will effect no real, vital, and lasting change in his habits, but will deliver him into a blind bondage to sin. If the feeling wears off, moreover, the individual may regard all religion as unreal . . . (p.10).

The Inner Code of Values Needs Reevaluation

What of the values we held before conversion? What of that code of behavior we had adopted but have repeatedly violated and have cursed ourselves for having violated? The code is still there, but we place it under close scrutiny. A large part of it we will recognize as valid. Much of the trouble has been in our violations of the code, not in the code itself. But at the same time, the code indeed may be defective. We will find it necessary to place the code itself under examination. It is at this point that we may find some of our greatest difficulty. The written word of God, the Bible must become the standard. It is there that the ultimate guiding principles will be found that will lead to the most abundant life.

While studying that book of instruction, the Bible, and the underlying principles of many of the recorded events, we may find that new "oughts" need to be adopted into the internal code book. And some of the old statutes may need to be updated or abandoned completely because they will be found to have no validity at all. Some that were adopted earlier may be found to be more harmful than good. Some may be found to have originated in parental or social bias with no worthy basis whatsoever. Remember Wanda who had been taught that she would be performing an immoral act by entering any building called a "church"? Some people alive today can remember when it was considered immoral for a woman to sit astride a horse.

New conflicts may arise at the point of departure from the formerly-held values. Remember that once a value is adopted by the internal legislator, it is difficult and sometimes almost impossible to repeal that statute. Keep in mind also that we have two levels at which we live – the thinking level and the feeling level. This is one more time that feelings and thoughts enter into conflict.

The woman mentioned earlier (Wanda) may be able to enter a church-building by telling herself that it is absurd to feel guilty for doing so. She may tell herself that it is also the good and right thing for her to do. But for a long time, possibly for the rest of her life, she may occasionally feel some pain of guilt feelings when she enters a church building because she is violating a statute that she adopted many years earlier. Entering a church building will turn on an old recording, calling forth the feeling of guilt. Like Pavlov's famous dog that became conditioned to salivate at the sound of a bell, she will have become conditioned to have feelings of guilt when entering a church building. But even Pavlov's dog, with time and experience, could be re-conditioned. With re-conditioning the dog would salivate only in the presence of good food. In the presence of ongoing love, with time and experience, Wanda can become re-conditioned to accept forgiveness so regularly that when she enters a church she will not experience the feelings of guilt.

All guilt feelings, whether real or unreal, normal or neurotic, if they are to be reduced constructively, they need to be canceled by the experience of forgiveness. This calls for more than just a one-time event. We need to experience it in an ongoing love relationship. Therefore, we speak of one living in a state of grace. That is, we live moment by moment in a relationship that accepts God's love that we have not merited.

But that love is experienced not only as God's forgiveness. Among other ways, it is experienced also as God's leadership. And the healthy response to His leadership is by obedience.

In obedience to known right, despite "conditioned" guilt, we may sometimes find it necessary to violate a formerly held value for the sake of the good of others or ourselves. Edward Stein, in his excellent old book, *Guilt: Theory and Therapy*, adds to this thought by saying:

The healthier and more mature the person, the more control is in the service of the values genuinely held, and the less the ideal is experienced as disadvantageous (except in moments of extreme temptation). There is identification with the good which relates duty to value rather than to the anxious avoidance of guilt. Duty to the value may even in some instances be prepared to run the risk of guilt or shame on behalf of the value. The more integrated the personality, the less conflict between the desired and the good (valued) occurs, because the good has come to be desired for itself rather than as a reluctant concession for the avoidance of guilt anxiety. Morality is consciously in control (p.80).

The morality that is consciously in control above all others is bound up in the one law given by Jesus -- the law of love: "You shall love the lord your God with all your heart, with all your soul , and with all your mind". . . and, "you shall love your neighbor as yourself" (Matt. 22:37-39). Upon this one statement hung all the law of both the Old and New Testaments; "Love one another." Again He summed up that law. "A new commandment I give to you, that you love one another even as I have loved you, you also must love one another" (John 13:34 NASB).

But no person does so to the fullest of his capacity. He fails. Therefore, he is guilty. And his inner judge does not let him forget it. Each time we declare ourselves "guilty," our response to that judgment will determine whether we move toward being cursed or blessed. We may turn from the grace of forgiveness, permitting ourselves to further harm ourselves, or we may use it as a voice calling us to forgiveness by a loving God. Accepted by God, we can say within ourselves, "If the King of the Universe accepts me with all my faults, who am I to reject me? If I am assured of His forgiveness I can forgive myself. I do not need to punish me."

Something else then is new. We have a fresh and healthier way of regularly coping with guilt, made possible by the ongoing daily relationship with God in the living, resurrected Jesus Christ.

Day by Day by Day

This daily aspect of life in a relationship with God is vital. A relationship is an ongoing experience and violations of expectations have a potential for damaging relationships again. But daily acceptance of forgiveness is essential also. Although ongoing forgiveness may not be deserved, it is offered; and he who refuses it turns from grace, the greatest of gifts.

We should keep in mind that Christ himself was a gift to humankind. "For God so loved the world, that He gave His only begotten Son, that whoever believeth in him should not perish, but have eternal life (John 3:16). A study of the Greek language, in which this passage of Scripture was originally written, reveals the word "believeth" is a continuous action verb, emphasizing that which goes on and on and on. In even so basic and often-quoted passage of scripture, the emphasis is given to the ongoing dailiness of the trusting relationship and the dailiness of the benefits of this trust (cf. Romans 5:10).

Having turned from self-idolatry and now devoted to the true God, aware of what God has done for us, we have a need to express adoration to that God. For this purpose, we gather in worship, to sing praises to Him for the abundant gifts of love that He has kept on lavishing upon us, His children. I refer to Christians as children because at the time we turned to Him in a trusting relationship, as we were made into new creatures, He adopted us (or begot us) as His own children. This body of people, called, "the church," gathers to adore the Father, and to speak with Him in the quiet communion of prayer, sing His praises and listen to His teachings. It becomes a time of reassurance -- a time of closer self-examination -- a time of more total commitment to the true God. It becomes a time of further release from the damning bond of guilt -- a time of further release from the former idolatrous devotion to the self -- and a time of mutual uplifting, each worshipper of the other.

A purpose of the church is to meet new, significant needs. A new life, with new values, new behavior, and new Center of Devotion may experience rejection from the people of former relationships. Among those still in the "cycle of the damned," an unspoken attitude often prevails: "Since you have departed from the way of destruction, I want nothing to do with you. We no longer walk the same path." Unspoken, even un-admitted, is the feeling, "Since I dare not admit the foolishness of my own self-destructive, degenerative behavior, I'll call you the 'fool' for going the straight life." The very presence of a righteous person serves as a prod to the conscience of the unrighteous who is reminded of where he is, as compared to where he ought to be. For this reason, the newly righteous may lose his former relationships.

The loss may include all former relationships; even father and mother, sister and brother. But God provides a body of people (the church) for fulfilling the deep psychological and social needs for primary relationships (cf. Ephesians 2:19). It is the task of the church to love, to woo, to entice, to enlist, to encourage, to feed, to befriend, to build, and to serve as a living, struggling community (family) of faith. It is a body of people who are living and loving, freed from the bondage of habitual sin; but never free from individual sins -- daily accepting the forgiving re-creative grace of God.

With the knowledge that we are still loved and accepted even when we fail, we find life richer and richer, more and more abundant. We can rejoice, singing, "I have Life. I'm free to live! If I fail, I'm still O.K. I'm still acceptable to God. And if I'm acceptable to Him, I'm acceptable to me. And if I'm acceptable to God and to me, I'm acceptable to God's people. At peace with the significant people in my world, at peace with God, and at peace with myself, I'm filled with joy -- the joy of being truly alive!" We have cause to celebrate. We celebrate life.

The potential for fulfillment and satisfaction on earth in a daily relationship with God in Christ is sufficient, in itself. Any further place, or state, or awareness of perfect existence is as dessert after a banquet. As we would attend a banquet even if we knew that there would be no dessert, benefactors of God's grace want the abundance of the banquet of the Christ-led life, even if there were no promise of Heaven. But we have a hope and promise of "all this and Heaven too!"

Because we are the happy recipients of God's abundance, we want to give of our abundance to others. And the "Law of love" requires it. We are at the heart of the call to evangelism. Essentially, evangelism is the act of inviting others to join us on our new pathway. Having been set free from the destructive bondage of our former attitudes and behavior by the life-changing love of God, we want to share with others. Enjoying the benefits of "all things new," we want to share with others! We want to share it with the spiritually blind who do not yet see the folly, the tragedy, and the damnation of paying the wages of sin that truly is death. But the gift of God is eternal life through Jesus Christ our Lord – our Savior (cf. Romans 6:23).

We are damned if we are not forgiven. Shout it! Speak it! Whisper it! "God loves you enough to forgive." Your family, friends, and acquaintances need to know it too. Hurry! Pass it on! Spread the Good News![2]

---

2 The word "Gospel" as used in the New Testament means "good news" – news so good that it is worthy of joyous celebration upon being heard.

Bibliography

Ashbrook, James A., 'The Impact of the Hospital' Situation in Our Understanding of God and Man" in Religion and Medicine, ed. David Belgum (Ames: Iowa State University Press, 1967).

Bruder Ernest E., *Ministering to Deeply Troubled People* (Englewood Cliffs: Prentice-Hall, 1963).

Coleman, James C., *Abnormal Psychology and Modern Life* (Glenville, IL: Scott Foresman, 1964).

Dobson, James, *Hide or Seek* (Old Tappan, NJ: Revell, 1974).

Ellis, Albert, *Reason and Emotion in Psychotherapy* (New York: Lyle Stewart,1962).

Emmerson, James G, Jr., *The Dynamics of Forgiveness* (Philadelphia: Westminster, 1964).

Frankl, Victor, *Man's Search for Meaning* (New York: Washington Square Press, 1963).

Freud, Sigmund, *Civilization and Its Discontents* (New York: W.W. Norton, 1961).

Fromm, Erich, *Escape from Freedom* (New York: Reinhart and Winston, 1941).

The Heart of Man (New York: Harper & Row, 1964).

Geaney, Dennis, *Living With Your Conscience* (Chicago: Thomas Moore Press, 1973).

Harris, Thomas, *I'm OK – You're OK* (New York: Harper and Row, 1967).

Hinsie, Leland E., and Campbell, Robert Jean, Psychiatric Dictionary 4th ed. (New York: Oxford University Press, 1970 Quoting Sigmund Freud, Inhibitions, Symptoms and Anxiety, 1936.

Horney, Karen, *The Neurotic Personality of Our Time* (New York: W.W. Norton, 1937).

Houselander, Caryll, *Guilt* (New York: Gordian Press, 1971).

Justice, Blair and Rita, *The Abusing Family* (New York: Human Sciences Press, 1976).

Justice, William G.,
Guilt and Forgiveness, (Grand Rapids, MI: Baker Book House, 1980).

Guilt: the Source and the Solution, (Wheaton, IL: Tyndale House Publishers, Inc., 1981).

A Ccmparative Study of the Language People Use to Describe the Personalities of God and Their Earthly Parents, (300N Zeeb Rd. Ann Arbor, MI: University Microfilms International, Doctoral Dissertation LD00963, 1984).

God in the Hands of Angry Sinners, (Bloomington, IN: 1st Books, 2004)

Kisker, George W., *The Disorganized Personality* (New York: McGraw-Hill, 1964).

LeVey, Anton S., *The Satanic Bible*, (New York: Avon Books, 1969).

Lewis, C.S., *Mere Christianity* (New York: Macmillan Paperbacks, 1960).

McAvoy, Hubert J.W., *Guilt, Atonement and Modern Culture* (Master of Sacred Theology dissertation, Oberlin College, 1950). Parentheses mine

Martin, William C., *These Were God's People* (Nashville: The Southwestern Co. 1966).

Mairet, Philip, ed. , *Christian Essays in Psychiatry*, (London: SCM Press, 1956).

Makers of the Modern Theological Mind, A multi-volume series (Waco, TX, 1970s & 1980s.)

Menninger, Karl,
  The Human Mind, 32nd ed. (New York: Knopf, 1959).

  Man Against Himself (New York: Harcourt, Brace and World, 1938).

  Whatever Became of Sin? (New York: Hawthorn Books, 1973).

Menninger, Walt,   *Rx for Crime*, The Knoxville News-Sentine/*16* July 1978, p.F-17.

Murphy, Carol, *Conscience and Psychotherapy*, Journal of Pastoral Care (No. 2, 1962).

Oates, Wayne E., *Confessions of a Workaholic* (Nashville: Abingdon, 1971).

Oden, Thomas C., *The Structure of Awareness* (Nashville: Abingdon, 1969).

Plato, *The Collected Dialogues,* Hamilton and Carnes, eds., Bellington Series 71 (Princeton: Princeton University Press, 1961).

Rokeach, Milton, *The Three Christs of Ypsilanti* (New York: Knopf, 1964).

Ross, Abraham Schwartz, *Modes of Guilt Reduction*, University of Minnesota, 1965. Order No. 65-15, 217. Abstracted in Social Psychology, p.4855, year unknown.

Stein, Edward V., *Beyond Guilt* (Philadelphia: Fortress Press, 1972), p.49.

Tawlinson, George, trans., and Manuel Komroff, ed., *The History of Herodotus* (NewYork: Tudor, 1944).

Tillich, Paul, *Systematic Theology; Vol. I   Reason and Revelation* (Chicago: University of Chicago Press, 1951).

Phillips, J.B., *Your God is Too Small*, (NewYork: The Macmillan Co., 1961).

Powell, Gordon, *Release from Guilt and Fear* (New York: Hawthorn, 1961).

Stein, Edward, *Guilt: Theory and Therapy*, (Philadelphia: Westminster Press, 1968).

Pusey, E.B., trans., *Confessions of St. Augustine*, (Mount Vernon: Peter Pauper Press, n.d.).

Tournier, Paul, *Guilt and Grace*, (New York: Harper, 1962).

Vincent, David, *Feel Free*, (New York: Dell, 1974).

Weatherhead, Leslie, *Psychology, Religion and Healing*, (New York: Abingdon Cokesbury, 1952).

Weihoten, Henry, *The Urge to Punish* (New York: Farrar, Straus and Cudahy, 1956).

Whitlow, Brian, *Hurdles to Heaven* (New York: Harper and Row, 1963).

Yancey, Philip, *What's So Amazing About Grace?* (Grand Rapids: Zondervan, 1997).

Index

About the Author

William G. Justice, D.Min, DPhil, DLitt, has authored eleven previous books and more than 200 articles. He has taught the Bible for more than fifty years, having begun while piloting B-29 Bombers for the U.S. Air Force during the Korean War. He listened to roughly 300,000 people at the bedside of his patients during the thirty-one years he ministered as a professional hospital chaplain. He has also listened for more than 20,000 hours as a Professional Counselor and a Marriage and Family Therapist (AAMFT).

The author has taught on-campus and off-campus extension courses for twelve colleges, universities, theological seminaries, and graduate schools. He chaired the Board of Governors of the Oxford Society of Scholars for sixteen years, and although retired, he still serves Oxford Graduate School as a Distinguished Professor of Religion and Sociey.

Damned If We Are Not Forgiven
Understanding Guilt and People Who Are Their Own Worst Enemies

GlobalEdAdvance Press
37321-7635
ISBN 978-0-9796019-9-6

www.ingramcontent.com/pod-product-compliance
Lightning Source LLC
Chambersburg PA
CBHW060252100426
42742CB00011B/1719